P9-CRJ-191

NEWCASTLE ISLAND

A PLACE OF DISCOVERY

BILL MERILEES

HERITAGE HOUSE

Copyright © 1998   William Merilees

CANADIAN CATALOGUING IN PUBLICATION DATA

Merilees, Bill
Newcastle Island

ISBN 1-895811-58-9

1.   Newcastle Island (B.C.)—History
I.   Title

FC3845.N49M47   1998   971.1'28   C98-910132-0
F1089.N49M47   1998

No part of this publication may be reproduced, stored in a retrieval system, or transmitted in any form or by any means—electronic, mechanical, photocopying, audio recording or otherwise—without the prior permission of Heritage House Publishing Company Ltd.

First Edition 1998

Heritage House wishes to acknowledge the support of Department of Canadian Heritage through the Book Publishing Industry Development Program, the Canada Council, and the Government of British Columbia for supporting various aspects of its publishing program through the British Columbia Arts Council.

Cover design: Cathy Mack
Book design and typesetting: Darlene Nickull
Front cover photos: Peter Schwarze, Schwarze Photographers, Nanaimo
Edited by: Joanne Richardson

HERITAGE HOUSE PUBLISHING COMPANY LTD.
Unit #8 - 17921 55th Ave., Surrey, BC V3S 6C4

Printed in Canada

Title page photo: Even in the 1890s Newcastle Island proved a remote but idyllic campsite. Here Mrs. Calvert Simpson's family camps near the Gap, with a kettle over the fire and guitars strumming.

DEDICATION

To John Cass, a cookie lover, whose knowledge of Nanaimo's history has helped uncover many fascinating stories. John's diligence and willingness to share his findings has added considerably to our understanding of Newcastle Island's wonderful past.

ACKNOWLEDGMENTS

From the time Newcastle Island first piqued my interest until the time this manuscript went to the publisher, a great many people have been very helpful: no one more so than John Cass. Over the 18 years this work has been in gestation, John continually provided me with material and ideas as well as insights into when events took place and where information could be found. On more than one occasion he made the long walk to my home with material in hand, had a cup of tea (and a cookie or two), and shared his knowledge of, and enthusiasm for, Nanaimo's early years.

Three more individuals were also very helpful. To Earl Marsh and Richard Mackie, for their research into the British Columbia Coast Steamship Service, and to Bill Munn (my one-time colleague at BC Parks), for his effort to better document the Japanese-Canadian saltery and shipbuilding operations, I owe a very special debt of gratitude. I am pleased to acknowledge their contribution to the main body of this history.

Behind the scenes were a great many dedicated professionals and their institutions, including:

Nanaimo Community Archives (NCA) (Diane Foster, Shirley Bateman, Joyce Command)

British Columbia Archives and Records Service (BCARS), Victoria (Brian Young, James Cline)

Vancouver Public Library (VPL)

Vancouver City Archives (VCA) (Ann Carroll, Carol Haber)

Provincial Archives of Manitoba, Hudson's Bay Company Archives, Winnipeg (Judith Hudson, Marie Reidke)

Vancouver Island Regional Library (Susan Yates, Meg Rintoule)

Snuneymuxw First Nation (Ellen White, Lorraine Littlefield)

Royal British Columbia Museum (Grant Keddie, Don Abbott)

BC Heritage Trust, Ministry of Small Business, Tourism and Culture
(John Stephenson, Doris Lundy)

Geographic Date BC, Ministry of Environment, Lands and Parks
(Janet Mason)

BC Parks, Ministry of Environment, Lands and Parks (Shirley
Derosiers, John Pinn, Jessie Carrick, Wayne Stetski)

Nanaimo's Wilf Hatch of Japan Cameras; Peter Schwarze of Schwarze
Photographers; and Scott Crawford of Courtenay, British Columbia, pro-
vided graphics. Individuals I want to recognize include Randy Fred, John
Allan, Alvin Fairhurst, Doreen Cowie, Marcia Galloway, Bob Bannerd
(Protection Island Ferries), Johnathan van der Goes (Newcastle Island
Ferries), David Fraser (Arenaria Research and Interpretation), Bob Turner,
Hugh Naysmith, Brian Grant, Andrew Merilees, Robert Spearing, Lynne
Bowen, the 1st Departure Bay Cub Pack, and Don MacIntosh.

I would also like to express gratitude to:

Nanaimo Historical Society (Ian and Daphne Paterson, Pamela
Marr)

Newcastle Island Pavilion Society (Gary Moore, Edna Arnold, Brian
Godfrey, Emil Sorensen, Merv Unger)

Nanaimo District Museum (Debbie Trueman, Debra Bodner)

BC Parks, South Vancouver Island District (Debbie Funk, Drew
Chapman, Dave Chater)

The Leon and Thea Koerner Foundation (Alice Macaulay)

Finally, and most important, I want to thank my wife June, who ques-
tioned, corrected grammar, and spell-checked more than one draft of this
publication.

As I look over this list (not to mention the years it has taken to bring
this project to fruition) and consider the hundreds of people with whom I
have had the pleasure of sharing Newcastle Island's incredible history, I
realize what an extensive and impressive network they comprise. What
stands out is the cheerful, friendly support and encouragement all these
people have provided. Can a simple "Thank you" ever be enough?

Bill Merilees,
Nanaimo, BC
January 1998

CONTENTS

INTRODUCTION

With the Nanaimo landscape and Mount Benson as its backdrop, Newcastle Island Provincial Marine Park helps define one of Vancouver Island's busiest harbours. Newcastle Island has a rich and varied history, a history that, in many respects, mirrors Nanaimo's development from a coal town to the sixth largest city in British Columbia, with a regional population of 100,000.

First Nations peoples arrived here 120 or more centuries ago. Along these shores they developed a rich, complex culture in tune with the seasons and the availability of natural resources. With a bountiful harvest at the water's edge, these ancestors of today's Coast Salish had little need to move far inland.

The arrival of a Spanish exploration party in 1792 heralded the coming of powerful foreign cultures that would all but eclipse Aboriginal ways of life. After the arrival of the Hudson's Bay Company (HBC), Nanaimo became an early outpost of Fort Victoria to the south. Driven by the discovery of coal in 1850, high-quality building materials (e.g., Douglas fir and sandstone), and rich stocks of herring and salmon, European, Chinese, and Japanese immigrants rapidly developed a new community motivated by trade and commerce.

In all the activities that spurred Nanaimo's growth, Newcastle Island played an important supporting role. Today, vestiges of earlier encroachments can be seen in many locations along the island's shores and trails. Fortunately, despite this, Newcastle Island has retained much of its natural grace. The sites modified by former human incursions are slowly but steadily being reclaimed by the forces of nature.

The purpose of this book is to put before the reader a simple, accurate account of Newcastle Island's history and to provide a suitable companion for any visitor to its shoreline. I have not attempted to fully develop each story; many await, and are worthy of, further research. It is in the interests of such research that I provide a list of references, copies of which are on file with the Nanaimo Community Archives and Nanaimo branch of the Vancouver Island Regional Library. All photographs, illustrations, tape recordings, and other materials gathered as part of this project have likewise been placed in these archival repositories. Readers who have materials or information that would be helpful to our further understanding of Newcastle Island's past are encouraged to add them to this record.

SOME SPELLINGS FOR NANAIMO

Snanaimuq—Franz Boas, 1889

Sne-ny-mo—John Thomas Walbran, 1909

Sneneymexw—Randy Bouchard, 1993

S'Na-Nay-Mos—From the story "Origin of the S'Na-Nay-Mos," by B. M. Cryer.

Nanymo—James Douglas, 1852

Nanaimo—Joseph Despard Pemberton, 1852

Ney-naimo—a term of endearment when Frank Ney was mayor of Nanaimo

Or—listen to a visitor try to work out the pronunciation when he or she first tries to pronounce Nanaimo.

Snuneymuxw—the current elders of the Nanaimo First Nation have adopted this as the name by which they wish to be known. Halkomelem linguists have not been able to determine either the origin or meaning of this word.

Num: 2

CARTA ESFÉRICA

de los Reconocimientos hechos en la Costa

DE AMÉRICA

en 1791 y 92. por las Goletas Sutíl y Mexicana
y otros Buques de S. M.

Nanaimo
Harbour

This Spanish map (c. 1795) shows a portion of the British Columbia and Washington State coasts as surveyed by Eliza, Galiano, and Valdes and possibly others. Note that both Gabriola, Newcastle, and many other gulf islands are not distinguished from Vancouver Island. Nanaimo Harbour is indicated as "Boca de Wintuisen." The bay where the Spanish anchored near Gabriola Island is indicated as Cala del Descanso.

CHAPTER 1

PLACE NAMES AND MAPS
—OFFICIAL AND UNOFFICIAL

The bedrock of Newcastle Island provides a geological history going back about 70 million years. Anthropologists have determined that First Nations peoples have resided here for around 12,000 years. The European presence in Nanaimo is only approaching 150 years. The home of the Snuneymuxw people, who had numerous seasonal villages along this shoreline, was defined by their pragmatic knowledge of the land and sea, both of which provided them with their means of sustenance. Though never mapped or recorded in European terms, the Snuneymux world was defined through oral history as passed down from generation to generation.

THE MAPS OF TWO CENTURIES

It was not until the late 1700s, with the arrival of British and Spanish exploration parties, that the shores of the Northwest Coast were charted. When the Spanish commanders Dionisio Alcala Galiano and Cayetano Valdes arrived off Gabriola Island in June 1792, their exploratory mapping included the entrance to Nanaimo Harbour. Though their work was published in 1802, it never gained the stature of Captain George Vancouver's charts and journals, which were published in 1798 and 1801, respectively. The map prepared by the Spanish named the harbour Boca de Wintuisen. They did not realize that channels separated Newcastle and Protection Islands from the main island, which they named Quadra y Vancouver.

The Spanish name for Vancouver Island resulted from an event that was already a decade old when their map was published. The signatures of Commander George Vancouver, RN, and "captain de navio" Don Juan Francisco de la Bodega y Quadra on the Nootka Convention of 1792 ended Spanish territorial aspirations on the Northwest Coast. To commemorate their meeting and friendly disposition towards each other, Vancouver named the island Quadra and Vancouver (in Spanish, Quadra y Vancouver).

This portion of Joseph Pemberton's 1853 map "Nanaimo Harbour and Part of the Surrounding Country" includes place names and hydrographic soundings. Note that Pemberton refers to Douglas Island, a name changed to Protection in 1853 according to Capt. Walbran. Joseph Despard Pemberton (insert), Surveyor General for Vancouver Island, 1851-1864, completed the first report, maps, and sketches of the Nanaimo area and the known coal deposits in 1852.

It was 1852 before employees of the HBC first charted Newcastle Island and the Nanaimo area, bestowing many place names, including Newcastle Island, as they went. With the discovery of coal, Joseph Despard Pemberton was dispatched to Nanaimo by HBC chief factor James Douglas who, in 1851, became governor of the British colony of Vancouver Island (he held the two positions of chief factor and governor until 1858). As the recently appointed surveyor general to the British colony of Vancouver Island, Pemberton surveyed and mapped the Nanaimo area. At least three of his maps showed Newcastle Island. These included several series of hydrographic observations and stand as the earliest known maps of the island.

The charting and mapping of our coast was continued between 1857 and 1863 by Captain George Henry Richards, RN, and between 1860 and 1870 by Master Daniel Pender, RN. However it was the work of Commander J. F. Parry, RN, and the British Admiralty's 1904 publication of the chart "Approaches to Nanaimo Harbour" that further refined Newcastle Island into the shape and proportions that we know today. All that remained to be added was the island's topography, which was completed in 1960 by Alvin Fairhurst of BC Parks, Engineering Section, Victoria. Interestingly, while Parry was completing his work, Captain John T. Walbran was completing his classic *British Columbia Coast Names, 1592-1906: Their Origin and History*.[1]

Along with the exploration parties and their maps came the naming of prominent features. In 1853 Newcastle Island itself was named by the officers of the HBC after the ancient coal city, Newcastle-upon-Tyne, in Northumberland, England. In all probability the Snuneymuxw had a Salish name for the island, but it has been lost.

Interestingly, in 1985, the Orienteering Association of British Columbia produced a map of Newcastle Island that combined facilities and topographic features along with selected information on geology and vegetation. This handy map became part of the 1985 British Columbia Summer Games Orienteering event program.

FIRST NATIONS PLACE NAMES

In the tradition of map-making on page 14 I have enclosed my own map of Newcastle Island—the first to document all the official and unofficial names mentioned in this chapter. The naming of locations has been a habit of humankind since time immemorial. On Newcastle Island, both official and unofficial place names may be traced to two specific periods in its history. The first is closely associated with the early Coast Salish, the second with the arrival of the Europeans.

*"Approaches to Nanaimo Harbour"—
Commander J. F. Parry, RN conducted
hydrographic surveys along the British Columbia coast between 1903
and 1906 while in command of Her Majesty's (Queen Victoria's)
Surveying Ship,* Egeria. *"Approaches to Nanaimo Harbour" was
completed in 1904. Note the stylized topographic elevations given to
Newcastle Island. The correct elevations only became known through a
topographic survey conducted under the direction of Alvin Fairhurst of
the BC Parks Branch in 1960.*

*Commander John F. Parry, RN (insert) was one of a number of officers
to command the* Egeria *with the purpose of continuing the pioneering
survey work of Captains Richards and Pender, 1857 to 1870.*

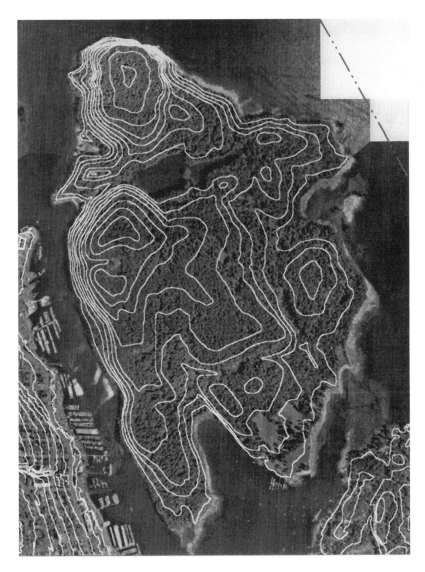

Satellite imaging map 1997—Produced in 1997 as part of the City of Nanaimo's planning process. Without anyone setting foot on the island, this map was produced strictly from aerial photographs by digital ortho-imaging.

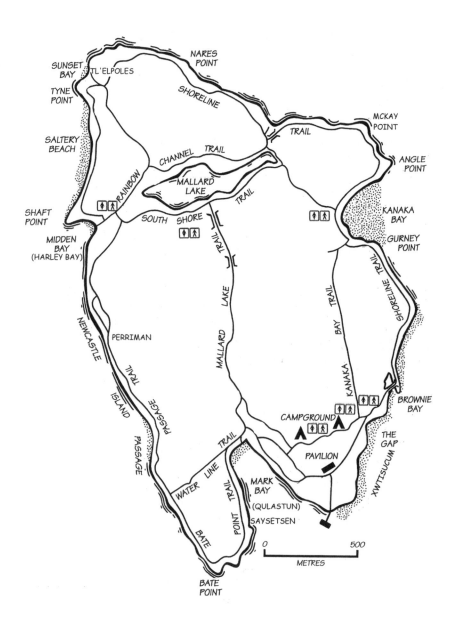

Newcastle Island Place Names

At the time of European contact it was the Snuneymuxw, a Coast Salish people, who occupied the greater Nanaimo area. These people had (and continue to have) a sophisticated culture, lifestyle, and language. Due in part to the oral nature of First Nations traditions, our current knowledge of their place names is based largely on memory and interpretation. During the past 150 years, their language has become increasingly dissipated, thus adding to the historian's challenge. Despite a concerted effort by the Snuneymuxw to research and establish traditional place names, our knowledge of these with regard to Newcastle Island is incomplete and, in some instances, contradictory.

It is believed that two village sites, Clostun and Saysetsen, were in use at the time of European contact. The Snuneymuxw moved from village site to village site on a seasonal basis, and it is impossible to determine exactly when any given site was abandoned for good.

Clostun, on the west side of Newcastle Island, is thought to have been located in today's Midden Bay. Translated, this name means "protector," an apt description for this secluded bay. A nearby village site, either a separate entity or possibly an extension of Clostun, was located along today's Saltery Beach facing Departure Bay (Ted Little, interview).

The ancient village site of **Saysetsen** sat at the foot of the long grassy slope facing towards Protection Island and Nanaimo Harbour. Archaeological evidence, gathered in 1976, indicates this site was in use about the time of European arrival (Ted Little, interview).

Three other Aboriginal place names are documented. **Qulastun**, a location near the head of Mark Bay, means "bay turned the wrong way." At the eastern entrance to The Gap (which separates Newcastle and Protection Islands) is a reef that is exposed during low tides. This reef was given the name **Xwtisucun**, meaning "to fasten" or "to anchor" (see photo in Chapter 10). In the Halkomelem dialect "tl'elp" means "deep," and a site known as **Tl'elpoles** was located between Tyne Point and Nares Point at Sunset Bay, where the deep-water channel enters Departure Bay. To the Snuneymuxw, this was noted as a good clam-digging area.

EUROPEAN PLACE NAMES

When Joseph Pemberton was despatched to survey the Nanaimo Harbour and environs, he gave Newcastle Island at least four place names: Boulder Point (near the island's northwest extremity and later renamed Nares Point), McKay Point (near the island's northeastern extremity), Point Mowatt (now Bate Point), and Angle Point. In his report to "James Douglas Esq, Gov. Vancouver's Island," Pemberton describes the Nanaimo area as having "Good soils, a cheerful aspect and very picturesque situation and the lands bordering upon the rivers and upon Departure Bay (which I so named from the circumstance of a large tribe of indians having lately abandoned it,[2] and from the probability of its affording a good exit to vessels bound outwards when the tide is flowing strongly) well fitted for agricultural purposes."[3] He also named Jesse Island.

Newcastle Island Passage the narrow channel between Nanaimo and Newcastle Island, is referred to as Exit Passage on Joseph Pemberton's 1853 map. The names Entrance Island, Exit Passage, and Departure Bay help us follow the course of early sailing vessels through Nanaimo Harbour. For these sailing vessels prevailing winds and tides were very important considerations when entering and/or leaving a port. Today the official place name is Newcastle Island Passage, not Newcastle Island Channel (as appears on many local maps). The name was changed from Exit Passage to Newcastle Island Passage on August 10, 1944, at the request of the Canadian Hydrographic Service, the latter being considered "more distinctive" than the former and avoiding duplication.[4]

Nares Point was originally identified as Boulder Point during Pemberton's 1852 survey. It was renamed by Captain Parry in 1903, after his surveying lieutenant, George Nares. The name Nares Point, being considered "a more distinctive name," was officially adopted by the Geographic Board of Canada on June 30, 1910.

The name **Tyne Point** is derived from the Tyne River and from the association of Newcastle Island with Newcastle-upon-Tyne. This name was originally applied in 1904 by Captain Parry during his resurvey of Departure Bay.

Shaft Point is a name that was adopted by the Geographic Board of Canada on June 30, 1910, and it is believed to have been chosen on the basis of its relationship to coal mining. The Fitzwilliam (and earlier the Newcastle) coal mine operated near this location from 1852 to 1883.

Bate Point is the long reef that extends southward into Nanaimo Harbour and marks the southern entrance to Newcastle Passage. First named Point Mowatt by Joseph Pemberton, then appearing as Reef Point on the British Admiralty Chart of 1862, it was finally named Bate Point by the Canadian Hydrographic Service in 1939. This final naming commemorates Mark Bate, JP, Nanaimo's first mayor and one-time manager of the Vancouver Coal Mining and Land Company.

Mark Bay is a name ignored by many long-time residents, who refer to this bay as "Echo Bay," a name that appears on Canadian Pacific Railway publications from the 1930s and that has been commemorated by a BC Parks sign for many years. The official name of Mark Bay, like that of Bate Point, also honours Mark Bate.

The name **Angle Point** appeared on Pemberton's 1853 map of "Nanaimo Harbour and Part of the Surrounding Country." But no explanation of why this name was chosen has survived. Angle Point was adopted formally by Captain George Henry Richards in 1862 and was published in the BC Gazetteer of 1930.

McKay Point recognizes a man instrumental in the founding of Nanaimo. Joseph William McKay was the HBC official instructed by Chief Factor James Douglas in 1852 "to proceed with all possible diligence to Wintuhuysen inlet, commonly known as Nanymo Bay [sic] and formerly take possession of the coal beds lately discovered."[5] It was McKay, during his fieldwork in 1850, who discovered an outcropping of coal near this location. McKay's service to the HBC and to the Colony of Vancouver Island (as a member of the first legislative assembly from 1855 to 1859) was exemplary. He died in 1900 at the age of 71.

UNOFFICIAL PLACE NAMES

Some of these, such as Echo Bay, are mentioned above. Over the years other names have appeared through the use of signs or by word of mouth. Both methods have brought certain names into popular usage.

During the early 1900s, prior to the First World War, the members of the Cowie family would take their launch to Newcastle and picnic at **Brownie Bay,** which they named in honour of a great aunt, Elizabeth Brownlow (Doreen Cowie, personal communication). BC Parks staff acknowledged this place name with a carved cedar sign shortly after the park's establishment.

Mark Bate is best remembered as the first mayor of Nanaimo. He was also the manager of the Vancouver Coal Mining and Land Company at the time the Newcastle and Fitzwilliam mines were in operation near Midden Bay in the 1870s.

A Cowie family picnic at Brownie Bay in 1925. People present—left to right—unknown, Reverend Welsh, Dora Cowie, Frank Cowie, Elizabeth Brownlow (Brownie), Lillian Cowie, unknown, Mrs. Welsh, unknown, unknown.

Kanaka Bay is infamous for the deeds of Peter Kakua. Peter was a Kanaka of Hawaiian descent who, with an axe, murdered four people in Nanaimo on December 3, 1869. He spent his last minutes of freedom at this secluded location. After being tried in Victoria and hanged in Nanaimo he was later buried at Kanaka Bay in an unmarked grave (see Chapter 7).

A short distance south of Kanaka Bay there is a very distinct fault scarp, or cleft, in the bedrock beside the trail. In his *The Geology of Nanaimo*, Bruce F. Gurney took the liberty to christen this location **Gurney Point**.[6]

Over the years a number of names have been used for the island's small, human-made lake, but **Mallard Lake** finally won out. Forerunners include Newcastle Lake, Beaver Lake, and Little Beaver Lake. The name "Beaver" probably goes back to the early 1930s, when the Canadian Pacific Railway introduced beaver and muskrat into the lake for the purpose of improving wildlife viewing. Since the British Columbia component of the *Gazetteer of Canada* lists no fewer than 15 Beaver Lakes,[7] BC Parks staff renamed it Mallard Lake around 1983 in order to reduce confusion. However, it may have been more appropriate to recognize a different bird, as respected naturalist Allan Brooks (1869-1946) found this lake to be a refuge for a substantial population of hooded mergansers (many of which ended up in his extensive bird collection). Perhaps Merganser Lake would have been more appropriate. Or, for that matter, Pumpkinseed Pond. The large numbers of pumpkinseed sunfish found in the lake ensures the presence of substantial flocks of mergansers and other fish-eating birds. How the Pumkinseed came to Mallard Lake is not known. In Canada, their natural habitat reaches only as far west as southeastern Manitoba. On Vancouver Island the introduction of small-mouthed bass is thought to have led to the introduction of the pumpkinseed sunfish as a bait species.

With the establishment of a sandstone quarry on Newcastle Island Passage, the workers' first task was to prepare the site. This led to the establishment of a small settlement named **Perriman**. The significance of this name appears not to have been recorded.

The name **Midden Bay** is derived from the substantive midden near the village site of Clostun. This cove saw considerable activity from the early 1850s to the close of the Fitzwilliam

James Harley was a resident at Midden Bay in the early 1930s.

coal mine in 1883. During the coal-mining period and, later, during the construction of a sewer discharge line across Newcastle Island to Rainbow Channel, the midden deposits at this designated archaeological site were substantially disturbed.

For some time before 1935, when a fire destroyed his small house, Jim Harley lived on Newcastle Island across from Brechin Point. His residence was known as **Harley Bay** for many years. A former chief jailer for the City of Nanaimo; a corporal (Imperial Light Infantry) in the Boer War; and, when required, a regimental chaplain, Jim had served his country and community in many capacities. After he lost all his possessions to fire on Newcastle Island his many friends pitched in to build and furnish a small house for him on Pine Street. Jim died February 6, 1936, at the age of 74. HarmAen Bay, a name shown on the Canadian Pacific Railway brochures of the 1930s, is possibly an error for Harley.[8]

Fitzwilliam Point is a name I proposed to commemorate the Fitzwilliam coal mine that operated at this location from about 1860 until 1883.

The Gap is the narrow shallow channel that separates Newcastle Island from Protection Island. Once a place where herring spawn was gathered by the Snuneymuxw people, The Gap remains a tricky passage only navigable by small boats at high tide.

Sunset Bay appropriately faces northwest and is ideal for watching sunsets. A shallow, cave-like overhang at the head of this bay, along with a nearby archaeological site, indicate that this feature possibly provided shelter for early First Nations inhabitants. In the 1930s local pioneer John Allan recalls that a hermit resided here, subsisting in part on fish taken with a small gillnet he moored just off-shore. This is the location of Tl'elpoles.

Saltery Beach is a name tied to the fishing industry. Japanese fishers used this long sand-gravel beach as a location for herring and salmon salteries. The activities within the salteries, as well as boat-building and vessel-repairing, took place from late in the nineteenth century until 1942, when all Japanese Canadians were sent to internment camps in the BC Interior and points further east.

The Gap as it appears today. Taken from Newcastle Island looking across to Nanaimo.

CHAPTER 2

GEOLOGICAL HISTORY

ORIGIN IN GEOLOGICAL TIME

As you walk the trails of Newcastle Island, the rocks under your feet provide little indication of their origins. They are the product of a complicated and fascinating geological history—remnants of the incredible processes of world plate tectonics, the movement of continents, and glacial scouring. The most informed theories suggest that the pre-history of Newcastle Island lies jumbled in the geological forces that resulted in the formation of Vancouver Island and the creation of western North America.[9] In the calendar that records geological time, changes take place over millions of years. Barring earthquakes, volcanic eruptions, tidal waves, or other forces of cataclysmic change, the variations we may see in one lifetime are hardly perceptible.

Newcastle Island, as we see it today, has changed little in the past 5,000 years. However, if we go back to the time the island's rocks were formed, then the story becomes quite interesting. Nearly all visitors to Newcastle Island are struck by the dramatic beauty of its sandstone shoreline. The sandstone and pebble rocks, called conglomerate, originated during the late Cretaceous period of Earth's history—about 80 million years ago. At this time the land mass of Vancouver Island had completed a remarkable journey of about 1,000 kilometres over a period of 83 million years. From a location somewhere off California, Vancouver Island (and the Queen Charlotte Islands) had drifted northward, carried along by the forces of plate tectonics, at a rate of about 1 centimetre per year. Eventually it literally bumped into western North America. The forces generated by this type of geological confrontation are immense, and during this collision the Earth's surface buckled, substantially elevating the mountain spine of Vancouver Island (including Mounts Benson and Arrowsmith). In addition, a broad basin developed along Vancouver Island's eastern slopes, extending from near present-day Campbell River southward. This is now known as the Nanaimo Lowland.

This basin, due to a mild climate, supported forest and swampland vegetation, and its eastern perimeter became the repository for sediments eroded from the nearby mountains. It is these materials that now make up the sandstone and conglomerate rock that underlie Newcastle Island (and all the sedimentary rocks from Campbell River southward, including the Gulf Islands). The vegetation, where deposited in sufficient bulk, eventually became compressed into the coal deposits that brought Nanaimo its mid-nineteenth-century prosperity.

After this great geological standoff, Vancouver Island entered a quiet period of erosion that lasted for the next 70 million years (until about 10 million years ago). Around this time volcanic activity created the rocky outcrops visible today in the Nanaimo highland above Departure Bay. If any volcanic rock was ever present on Newcastle Island it has disappeared through the never-ending process of erosion.

About two million years ago the great ice ages began, and they were to define the surface texture of Western Canada. On three occasions during this time tremendous rivers of ice flowed from the Vancouver Island and Coast mountains to converge in Georgia Strait. At times more than a mile thick, these rivers flowed southward over the Nanaimo Lowlands and into the Pacific Ocean via Juan de Fuca Strait. During this process hundreds of metres of sediment were scraped from the basin's surface and carried away. The tremendous weight of the ice depressed land surfaces, pushing them downward by as much as 300 metres. After the ice rivers finally retreated, Vancouver Island's surface appeared as a battlefield of gouges and grooves tending in a southeasterly direction. Scattered about were boulders (known as glacial erratics) and ridges of glacial till. These boulders of predominately crystalline rock—granite and granodiorite—are located outside the Nanaimo Lowland area, with most coming from the mountains of the present-day Mainland.

Thirteen thousand years ago, when the last ice finally melted away, Newcastle Island remained submerged under about 120 metres of water. It was not until the Earth's surface began its slow rebound from the weight of the ice that the land features we now recognise as greater Nanaimo emerged from beneath the sea.

According to geological surveys of Canada, 65 million years ago, during the Upper Cretaceous period, 7,600 feet of sediment were deposited in this area. The youngest of these deposits is the Gabriola Formation and the oldest is the Benson Formation. Since that time, erosion has al-

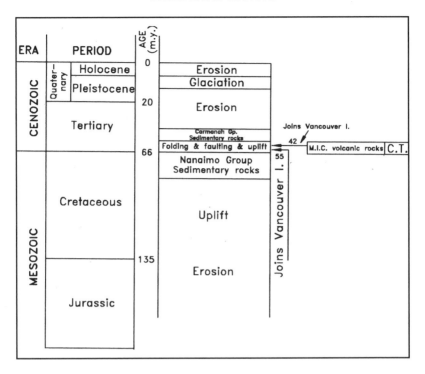

ERA	PERIOD		AGE (m.y.)			
CENOZOIC	Quaternary	Holocene	0	Erosion		
		Pleistocene		Glaciation		
			20	Erosion		
	Tertiary				Joins Vancouver I.	
				Carmanah Gp. Sedimentary rocks	42	
			66	Folding & faulting & uplift	55	M.I.C. volcanic rocks C.T.
MESOZOIC	Cretaceous			Nanaimo Group Sedimentary rocks	Joins Vancouver I.	
				Uplift		
			135	Erosion		
	Jurassic					

Geological time scale indicating the late Cretaceous origin of the Nanaimo sedimentary rock formation.

tered the landscape dramatically. The exposed rock surfaces seen on Newcastle Island today come from near the bottom strata of this series, signifying that much of the original sediment has been eroded. In fact, none of the five top layers of sediment has survived on Newcastle. A minimum of two-thirds (5,000 feet) of the sediment have been scraped away, leaving only three of the original eleven distinct formations visible. The youngest layers of sediment, seen south from about Mallard Lake, represent the fine-grained sandstone of the Protection Formation. The historic building-stone and pulp-stone quarry sites of Newcastle Island were blasted into this strata. The Newcastle Formation, which contains the Newcastle and Douglas coal seams, is one layer older than the sandstone outcrops. The seams occur as a band stretching across Newcastle Island from Shaft Point towards McKay Point. North of this, conglomerate rocks of the Protection Formation are easily seen and were actually documented on Dr. James Hector's 1860 map (see sidebar and illustration). This profile shows the north-south sequence of these three sedimentary formations, although the delineation and naming of these layers came much later.

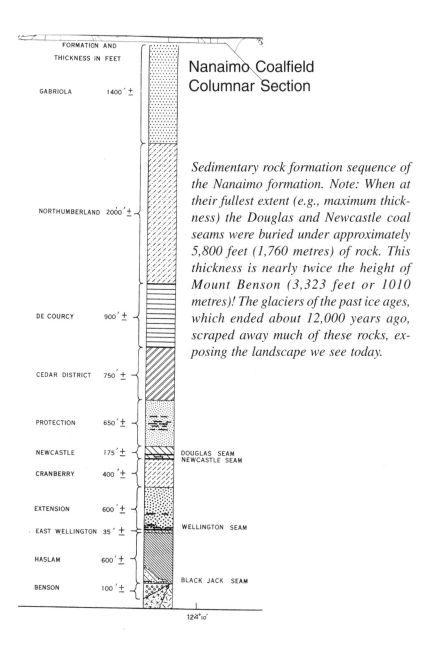

FORMATION AND
THICKNESS IN FEET

Nanaimo Coalfield
Columnar Section

FORMATION	THICKNESS
GABRIOLA	1400' ±
NORTHUMBERLAND	2000' ±
DE COURCY	900' ±
CEDAR DISTRICT	750' ±
PROTECTION	650' ±
NEWCASTLE	175' ±
CRANBERRY	400' ±
EXTENSION	600' ±
EAST WELLINGTON	35' ±
HASLAM	600' ±
BENSON	100' ±

Sedimentary rock formation sequence of the Nanaimo formation. Note: When at their fullest extent (e.g., maximum thickness) the Douglas and Newcastle coal seams were buried under approximately 5,800 feet (1,760 metres) of rock. This thickness is nearly twice the height of Mount Benson (3,323 feet or 1010 metres)! The glaciers of the past ice ages, which ended about 12,000 years ago, scraped away much of these rocks, exposing the landscape we see today.

DOUGLAS SEAM
NEWCASTLE SEAM

WELLINGTON SEAM

BLACK JACK SEAM

124°10'

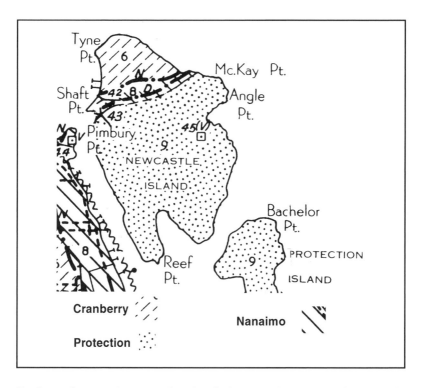

Geological map of Newcastle Island showing, from top to bottom, the location of the Cranberry, Newcastle, and Protection sedimentary formations. The dash-dot lines indicate the Newcastle and Douglas coal seams.

In the Nanaimo area the ancient rock formations have been altered primarily by a strong series of geological faults crossing the area from northwest to southeast. Newcastle Island Passage, for example, owes its creation to the faulting process. Today, Newcastle strollers can see a second observable fault-line along Shoreline Trail at Gurney Point, a short distance south of Kanaka Bay. Here a fault scarp (a distinct cleft) drops abruptly from the trail some 10 metres to the beach.

Not all the rock seen on Newcastle Island is of sedimentary origin. Although all the bedrock is sedimentary, glaciers have left behind tons of exotic material. Boulders of igneous rock types (e.g., andesite, granite, and granodiorite) are visible along various beaches and may be identified by their crystalline structure. The best place to observe these rocks is along the island's northeast shore.

Diagrammatic longitudinal section of Newcastle Island from Dr. Hector's geological report, indicating the type of sedimentary rock present and the location of the coal seams. Note: This diagram was prepared in 1860, long before the geological formations had been studied and named. Dr. Hector was part of the Palliser Expedition of 1857 to 1860.

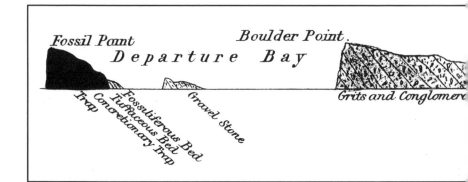

DR. JAMES HECTOR

Newcastle Island's early importance to Vancouver Island was tied to coal. And it was that coal that periodically attracted the interest of some of the great personalities of BC history.

One of the earliest of these personalities was Dr. James Hector, the geologist on the original British North America Exploring Expedition of 1856-60 headed by John Palliser. Hector was a hardy Edinburgh medical doctor, naturalist, and geologist, and he made a major contribution to the early geological knowledge of the Canadian west.

Near the end of this overland expedition that had scaled and identified major passes through the Rockies, Hector arrived in Victoria on January 16, 1860. Almost immediately he was despatched by canoe to Nanaimo and Newcastle Island to examine coal structures. His comprehensive work, completed within a very limited period of time, is enhanced by his sketches of the mining operations on Newcastle Island.

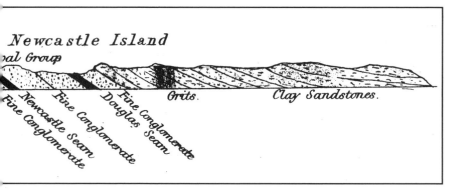

27

The Devil's Kitchen is a good example of fretted (sculptured) sandstone seen at Newcastle Island. Good examples of this type of weathering can been seen along Newcastle Island Passage.

Chapter 3

The Snuneymuxw

It is not known when the first humans arrived in the vicinity of Newcastle Island. Theories strongly suggest that the original First Nations people arrived in North America via a land-bridge that spanned the Bering Strait. Whether these people then travelled southward via an ice-free corridor through the BC Interior, via an oceanic route, via a broad coastal plain, or via island hopping is still being debated. Whatever the means, archaeologists believe that at least 11,000 years ago people had reached southwestern British Columbia.

For the Nanaimo area, little archaeological/ethnological research has been completed on early First Nations cultures. However, evidence gathered at Departure Bay indicates that this site has been continuously occupied for at least 2,000, and possibly as many as 4,000, years.[10] The First Nations people in the Nanaimo area wish to be known by the name Snuneymuxw (sn-nigh-mo). The Snuneymuxw have a number of myths that account for their origin. These stories tell that the Sun created and placed the first people on the slopes of Mount Benson. From the mountainside these people made their way down to Departure Bay, where they started a village and then extended their residency both northward and southward.

In 1792 Spanish captains Galiano and Valdez became the first Europeans to make contact with First Nations people when, on June 14, 1792, they dropped anchor in Descanso Bay, Gabriola Island. At one time during their visit the Spanish schooners were surrounded by 39 canoes, each carrying two or three First Nations people. J. T. Walbran wrote that

The Snuneymuxw villages around Nanaimo harbour were similar to this Salish settlement near Comox.

"Snenymos" (his spelling) meant "big strong tribe."[11] The name "Nanaimo" is derived from "Snenymos." Anthropologist Franz Boas records that, formerly, these people were very warlike.[12]

The Snuneymuxw territory included Nanaimo Harbour as far north as Neck Point, Gabriola Island, and the Nanaimo River watershed and as far south as Boat Harbour. Newcastle Island was within this territory and contained two village sites, Clostun and Saysetsen, both apparently un-occupied at the time coal was discovered in 1850. Other locations on Newcastle Island were important food gathering and resource procure-ment locations.

The Snuneymuxw were composed of five clans, each with a chief. In times of war, these clans would amalgamate and a war chief would lead all the warriors of the tribe. Contrary to a commonly held belief it was not the Haida from the Queen Charlotte Islands with whom the Snuneymuxw waged war. During the early half of the nineteenth century it was the Lekwiltok tribes of the Kwakwaka'wakw nation (Southern Kwakiutl)[13] who were their enemy. These people were also known as the Yaculta or the Euclataw. One major tribal battle occurred near Kelsey Bay around 1849, and the Snuneymuxw, despite losing many warriors, were victorious. The next year, near Maple Bay, a combined Salish force again defeated the Lekwiltok.[14]

The Snuneymuxw are part of the Coast Salish linguistic group, whose territory extended as far north as Kelsey Bay and as far south as Puget Sound. The Salish were further divided according to dialect. The Snuneymuxw dialect—Halkomelem—was shared with the Nanoose, the Chemainus, the Cowichan, and groups along the lower Fraser River.

Like many First Nations groups, the Snuneymuxw maintained a regu-lar pattern of seasonally dictated relocations. In April they moved from their winter village at Departure Bay to False Narrows on Gabriola Is-land to gather clams and camas bulbs, to fish for cod and grilse, and to hunt seals and sea lions. In August they moved to the mouth of the Fraser River to fish the early Sockeye and Pink salmon runs. They then returned to the Nanaimo River in time to fish the Chum salmon run.[15] After this, they returned to their winter village at Departure Bay, which they occu-pied from December until April, when the cycle would be repeated. It was at Departure Bay that they celebrated their winter dances and other spiritual and artistic pursuits.

When the Snuneymuxw relocated they took with them the large cedar boards used to construct the walls and roofs of their houses. To the un-knowing, this often gave the appearance that village sites had been permanently abandoned when, in fact, they had not. The Snuneymuxw presence on Newcastle Island is documented at twelve archaeological sites of undetermined age. All are fully protected, and it is a serious offence to disturb or tamper with them in any way. Surprisingly, considering the great number of petroglyphs in the Nanaimo area, there are no known petroglyphs on Newcastle Island.[16]

The Snuneymuxw used many of the island's resources to sustain their lifestyle. One very important resource was herring, which spawned around the island during late winter and early spring. Immense quantities of herring spawn were collected from the shallow passage between Newcastle and Protection Islands. Here cedar boughs were laid down at low tide and, later, the spawn, which was deposited on the branches, was stripped, dried, and stored for winter use.[17]

Cedar bark was another resource collected on Newcastle Island. If one looks carefully, along the trail between Giovando Lookout and the former sewer outfall into Rainbow/Fairway Channel one will see Western red cedar trees that have been culturally modified by stripping.

Randy Boucard mentions Newcastle Island, along with Protection Island, as an important deer-hunting and shellfish-gathering area.[18] Inland from Kanaka and Mark Bays stands of scouring rush (*Equisetum hyemale*) were gathered for use as an abrasive to smooth and polish various surfaces.[19]

A stripped cedar along Newcastle trail documents a First Nations presence.

The mortuary customs of the Snuneymuxw varied according to individual status. Traditionally, the face of the deceased was painted red and black and the corpse put into a box, which was then placed on four posts about five feet above the ground. The degree of carving and ornamentation on the box and poles indicated the deceased's rank. On rare occasions mortuary boxes were fastened to the tops of trees. Boas does not discuss the use of caves as the final resting place for mortuary boxes, but the caves and galleries at the north end of Newcastle Island were known repositories. Snuneymuxw oral history tells us, however,

THE CANNIBAL ROCKS

Along the northeast corner of Newcastle Island are a number of large shoreline rocks that could easily be identified as sentinals or lookouts. These rocks are considered to be *hamatsa* or cannibal beings, powerful spiritual images of the Euclataw. The *hamatsa* ceremony, long associated with ritual cannibalism and the most secret of the winter dances, is a documented rite of the Nuu-chalnulth and northern coastal tribes, including the Kwakwaka'wakw, the Haida, and the Tsimshian.

Franz Boaz traced the original concentration of villages that practised ritual cannibalism to the Heiltsuk people in the Rivers Inlet area. Any myths attached to a *hamatsa* image existing on Newcastle Island are likely attributable to the Euclataw, as there is no known record of the *hamatsa* ceremony among the Coast Salish peoples.

that these "Necrophiles of the Dead," as they were described by area resident Mark Bate, were not Salish but Lekwiltok, or Euclataw. Quite a number of Euclataw came south to Nanaimo to find employment with the HBC after coal mining at Fort Rupert ceased in 1852. "Euclataw Ranch," as their village was known, was scattered, some people living near the mouth of the Millstone River, others living along Newcastle Island Passage. And some are said to have camped on Newcastle Island, where their dead were placed in the aforementioned caves (Nanaimo First Nation Treaty Negotiation Office, personal communication). Mark Bate formally complained about this to Governor Douglas and requested that these remains be given a Christian burial. An order to this purpose was given in 1862.

Sustained warfare with the Lekwiltok, along with major smallpox epidemics in 1782 and 1862, respectively, susbstantially reduced the Snuneymuxw population at the time European occupation was expanding. Whether these or other events dictated the final abandonment of the village sites of Clostun and Saysetsen remains unclear. Today, all that can be identified at these archaeological sites is what remains of kitchen middens—dark brown to black soil heavily laced with clam shell.

Old Man Rock
Nanaimo, B.C.

Kayakers, recreational boaters and BC Ferry passengers out of Departure Bay get the best viewpoints of Old Woman rock (c. 1925) and Old Man rock (c. 1930) as they stand off the northeast coast of Newcastle.

THE TRANSFORMER

Salish people have long recognized the powers of a supernatural being, or spirit capable of transforming humans into rock formations.

The sandstone of Newcastle and other gulf Islands yield assorted evidence of these incredible powers.

WHAT IS A MIDDEN?

"Midden" is a word of Scandinavian origin, meaning dung heap or manure pile. In an archaeological context, midden refers to a refuse heap—especially to a refuse heap composed of kitchen wastes.

Along the Northwest Coast extensive middens, the largest covering many hectares, were associated with village sites. Smaller middens indicate the locations of short-term or seasonal habitation. Midden accumulations were dominated by clam shells which, due to high calcium content, establish a high pH factor in the surrounding soil. This alkaline condition is most attractive to archaeologists, as it is favourable to the preservation of organic materials such as wood, antler, bone, and some plant remains.

JOHN CASS

Few people have explored more facets of the early life and times of Nanaimo than John Cass. Born in Nanaimo in 1921, John had a variety of occupations before joining the Black Ball Ferry Company's (forerunner of BC Ferries) Catering Department in 1953. When Black Ball became part of British Columbia's ferry system, John spent the remainder of his 32-year career in coastal service. His final years were spent on the *Queen of the North*.

John's father was a coal miner at the Protection Island mine, a fact that led to John's interest in Nanaimo coal-mining history. From 1968 to 1980 John scripted local history stories for CHUB Radio. From 1962 onward his "Remember When" and "The Way It Was" series in the *Nanaimo Free Press* touched just about every subject imaginable regarding Nanaimo's past. John has revisited virtually every back issue of the *Nanaimo Free Press* since 1874 as well as many issues of Victoria's *British Colonist*.

With regard to Newcastle Island, John's series of notes and references relating to the operation of the sandstone quarry have been extremely helpful.

CHAPTER 4

THE ROLE OF COAL

In the 1830s and 1840s steam power was beginning to supersede sail power on the oceans of the world. With regard to the vessels comprising the British fleet, coal from England could power them to Chile, where the coal fields near Valparaiso could then replenish their supply. A source of good quality coal on the Northwest Coast was much sought after, as it would be of immense value to the British fleet and to other steam-driven ships.

Well before the discovery of coal at Nanaimo, the HBC recognized the potential advantage of a steam-powered trading vessel on the Northwest Coast. Dr. John McLaughlin, chief factor at Fort Vancouver (Washington), was quoted as saying that "a steam vessel would afford [the HBC] incalculable advantages over the Americans."[20] In 1835 the SS *Beaver* was launched in England. The *Beaver*, at 187 tons and 101 feet long (30.7 metres), had the capacity to be powered by both sail and steam. Under sail it arrived at Fort Vancouver in 1836, where it was converted to steam power, thus becoming the first steamship on the west coast. The *Beaver* burned 700 pounds of coal per hour. Until coal was discovered at Nanaimo, this fuel was delivered by sail. Frequent visitors to Nanaimo, the *Beaver* and its companion the *Otter* are among the legendary vessels of early BC maritime history. The *Beaver*'s career came to an end when it ran aground at Brockton Point in Burrard Inlet in 1888.

In 1835 small amounts of coal had been found on northern Vancouver Island at Fort Rupert, but the seams were narrow and the coal was not of good quality. When James Douglas became chief factor at Fort Victoria, locating a new source of coal was a top priority.

A group of Snuneymuxw, c. 1860. The older man in the middle, barefoot and with a walking stick, is Che-wech-i-kan, the person who first reported the presence of coal in the area of Wintuhuysen Inlet to the Hudson's Bay Company in December 1849. For his discovery he became know as Coal Tyee, or "Great Coal Chief."

THE DISCOVERY

Peaceful and serene are words appropriate to Wintuhuysen Inlet (now Nanaimo Harbour) before a Snuneymuxw, Che-wech-i-kan, arrived at the HBC blacksmith shop at Fort Victoria to have his gun repaired. While there, he observed coal being used to replenish the smith's fire and mentioned that there was plenty of such stone where he lived. This information was passed on to Joseph McKay, a company clerk, who then told Che-wech-i-kan that if he brought some pieces of the stone to Fort Victoria then he would receive a bottle of rum and have his gun repaired for nothing. In April of 1850 Che-wech-i-kan brought a canoe loaded with what proved to be a fine quality coal.

Upon hearing this information, James Douglas instructed McKay to accompany Che-wech-i-kan and investigate the source of this discovery.

They reached Che-wech-i-kan's home village in early May and, a week later, located a thick seam of coal in a narrow cove close to where Nanaimo's landmark Bastion rests today near the city harbour. Narrower seams were also located on Newcastle Island. These discoveries changed the complexion of this quiet inlet forever. For his discovery, Che-wech-i-kan became known as "Coal Tyee" or Great Coal Chief. Coal seams on Newcastle Island are still visible today. A three-inch seam can be seen on the beach on the east side of the island, and a 20-inch seam outcrops west of McKay Point and crosses the island to appear again above Saltery Beach.

Joseph McKay, Company Clerk for the Hudson's Bay Company at Fort Victoria. It was in this capacity that he accompanied Che-wech-i-kan to Wintuhuysen Inlet in May of 1850—a vist that led to the "formal" discovery of the Nanaimo coal fields.

Although McKay reported his findings to Douglas, the latter was still hoping that exploration efforts at Fort Rupert would fulfil the HBC's needs. Only in 1852, nearly two years after McKay's report, did Douglas turn his attention to Wintuhuysen Inlet. Following a personal inspection Douglas enthusiastically reported to HBC headquarters in August 1852 that very satisfactory results had been obtained and that in a single day, with the assistance of First Nations people, the company procured about 50 tons of coal at the cost of 11 pounds paid in goods.

Douglas had no doubt about the importance of this discovery. He decided to take immediate possession of the area in the name of the HBC and to commence development without delay. Joseph Pemberton, the HBC surveyor, was sent to assist with this acquisition. His report of September 27, 1852, adopted a variation of the First Nations name, "Snuneymuxw," for his location; and so Wintuhuysen Inlet became Nanaimo Harbour.

Initially, coal-mining developments took place on Vancouver Island proper. Only after Boyd Gilmour and other miners transferred to Nanaimo from the unsuccessful workings at Fort Rupert did the coal seams on Newcastle Island receive attention.

Douglas's letter to McKay:[21]

Fort Victoria, 24 August 1852
Mr. Joseph McKay
Sir:

You will proceed with all possible diligence to Wintuhuysen Inlet, commonly known as Nanymo [sic] Bay and formally take possession of the Coal beds lately discovered there for and in behalf of the Hudson's Bay Company.

You will give due notice of that proceeding to the Masters of all vessels arriving there and you will forbid all persons to work the coal either directly by means of their own labour or indirectly through Indians or other parties employed for that purpose except under the authority of a license from the Hudson's Bay Company.

You will require for such persons as may be duly licensed to work coal by the Hudson's Bay Company, security for the payment of a royalty of 2/6 a ton which you will levy on the spot, upon all Coal whether procured by mining or by purchase from the natives, the same to be held by you and from time to time duly accounted for.

In the event of any breach or evasion of these regulations you will immediately take means to communicate intelligence of the same to me.

I remain Sir

Your obed't servt.

James Douglas

After James Douglas visited Nanaimo he sent both Joseph McKay and his cartographer north from Fort Victoria.

Joseph Pemberton's first map of the Nanaimo area (below) was prepared in 1852. This map accompanied his September 27, 1852, report to James Douglas. Note on the north shore of Newcastle Island that Pemberton indicates "Coal Sect. 5."

The sketch of the coal seam sequence was also included in Pemberton's report to Douglas. Its location was just west of McKay Point.

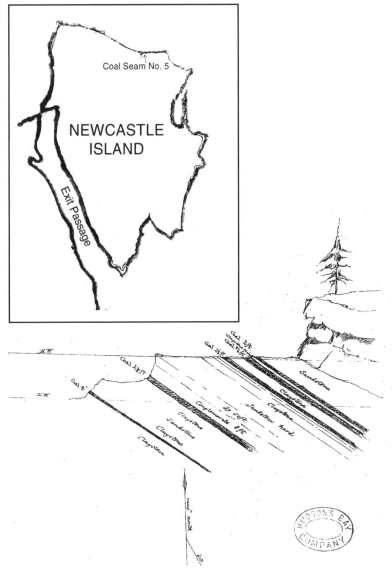

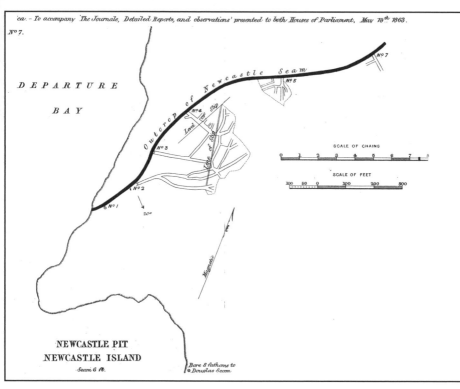

ca. - To accompany 'The Journals, Detailed Reports, and observations' presented to both Houses of Parliament, May 19th 1863.

Nº 7.

DEPARTURE

BAY

Outcrop of Newcastle Seam

Nº 7

Nº 5

Nº 4

Level of Slip

Line of Slip

Nº 3

Nº 2

Nº 1

20°

Magnetic

NEWCASTLE PIT
NEWCASTLE ISLAND
Seam 6 ft.

Bore 8 fathoms to
Douglas Seam.

SCALE OF CHAINS

0 1 2 3 4 5 6 7 8

SCALE OF FEET

100 50 0   100   200   300

Newcastle Mine map—Dr. Hector's report to "both Houses of (the British) Parliament, May 19th, 1863" as part of the British North American Exploring Expedition, 1857 to 1860 (aka the Palliser Expedition) contained this map of the workings of the Newcastle mine (pit) as recorded in 1860. Note: What would become the Fitzwilliam mine is indicated by "Bore 8 fathoms (48 feet or 14.6 metres) to Douglas seam."

This 1862 photo of coal ships at the wharf near Nanaimo's Bastion was the only known photo of Nanaimo taken by Francis G. Claudet. The photo was preserved by his son, Frederick Claudet of Nanoose Bay, BC.

The mining operations as they appeared above Midden Bay on June 14, 1875. Nearly 30 buildings are visible. The foundations of the building with the stone chimney (left of centre) can still be seen. Note: There is a dugout canoe of Indian design in the bay. These canoes were what were most often used for transportation.

THE PALLISER EXPEDITION

Although named for its commander, Captain John Palliser, the formal designation for this expedition was the British North American Exploring Expedition, 1857 to 1860. It was sponsored by the Royal Geographical Society (London, England) and funded by the Her Majesty's (Queen Victoria's) Government. The purposes of the expedition were:

1. To survey the watershed between the Saskatchewan and Missouri Rivers
2. To explore the Rocky Mountains and to ascertain the most southerly pass to the Pacific Ocean within British territory
3. To report on the natural features and general capabilities of the country
4. To construct maps of routes taken and prepare reports on the surveys undertaken

Interestingly, James Hector, the expedition's geologist, was asked by Sir Roderick Murchison, President of the Royal Geographical Society, to examine and report on the coal strata of Vancouver Island.[22]

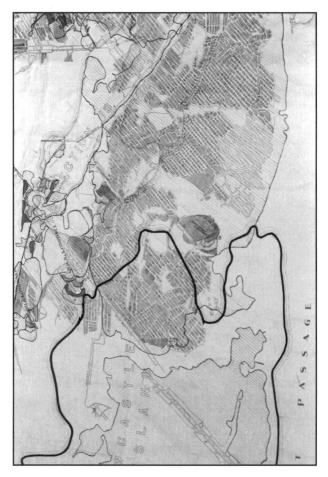

The mining conducted underneath Newcastle Island operated on the pillar and stall method. This map provides an indication both of the maze of tunnels and pillars that were present hundreds of feet underground and the extent to which mining had proceeded. Note: There is a convergence of two separate mining operations: the Protection or Number 1 mines from the south and the Brechin mine from the northwest.

Advertisement (reproduced right) that appeared in the British Colonist *newspaper (c. 1862) regarding the availability of shares in the Vancouver Coal Mining Company Limited. The names of the directors read like a "who's who" of Nanaimo street names. The main destination of Nanaimo coal was San Francisco.*

VICTORIA ADVERTISEMENTS

THE
VANCOUVER COAL MINING CO.,
LIMITED

Incorporated under the Joint Stock Companies' Acts, 1856 and 1857, whereby the Liabilities of the Shareholders are limited to the amount of their Shares.

Capital, £100,000 in 10,000 Shares of £10 Each

DEPOSIT £1 per Share on application, and £1 10s. on Allottment.

DIRECTORS

HON. MR. JUSTICE HALIBURTON, M.P., Chairman of the Canadian Land and Emigration Company.

GEORGE CAMPBELL, ESQ., (H.N. Dickson & Co., London; Dickson, Campbell & Co., Victoria, V.I.; Dickson, DeWolf & Co., San Francisco.)

HON. C.W. WENTWORTH FITZWILLIAM, M.P., Alwalton, Peterborough.

JOSEPH FRY, ESQ., (Messers. Trueman & Fry, Gresham House) Director of the Canada Agency Associations.

JAMES V.H. IRWIN, ESQ., F.R.G.S., 7 Hereford Square, South Kensington.

PRIDEAUX SELBY, ESQ., 4 Lowndes Street, Director of the Canada Agency Association.

Solicitors—Messrs. FRESHFIELDS & NEWMAN, Bank Buildings.

Bankers—Messers. ROBARTS, LUBBOCK & Co., London; THE CHARTERED BANK OF BRITISH COLUMBIA AND VANCOUVER ISLAND, Victoria.

Broker—C.W. PRICE, Esq., 54 Threadneedle Street

Secretary—H. WINFIELD GRACE, Esq.

Offices—16 Gresham House, Old Broad Street.

Resident Manager of Nanaimo—C.J. NICHOL, Esq.

DICKSON, CAMPBELL & CO., Agents, Wharf St.

DICKSON, CAMPBELL & CO.,
COMMISSION MERCHANTS,

Store Street, Victoria

H.N. DICKSON & CO., ... 3 George Yard, Lombard Street, London

DICKSON, DE WOLF & CO., ... San Francisco.

COAL MINING ON NEWCASTLE ISLAND

In January 1853 James Douglas employed Boyd Gilmour to sink another shaft on Newcastle Island. Gilmour believed that a 7-foot seam of coal would be struck at a depth of 30 fathoms (180 feet, or 55 metres). At seven fathoms Gilmour ran up against conglomerate rock, whereupon, for all of two days, he abandoned the idea of making Newcastle Island a mining site. Joseph McKay, then in charge of the overall coal project, had found another coal seam across the channel, near the mouth of the Millstone River. This seam looked very similar to the one he had found previously at McKay Point. Further work by an optimistic McKay determined that his original seam crossed Newcastle Island and outcropped in a cliff facing Departure Bay. Gilmour, however, remained discouraged. Meanwhile, back in Victoria, Douglas was concerned about the vacillating opinions regarding the feasibility of establishing a mine site on Newcastle Island.

In August 1853 Douglas determined that there were three workable coal-mining locations in the Nanaimo area—the site of the original discovery on Nanaimo Harbour, a site on Protection Island, and a site at Midden Bay on Newcastle Island. At each of these sites the highly faulted nature of the coal seams made it difficult for the miners to determine the best methods to use and the best coal beds to use them on. Nowhere was this more of a dilemma than on Newcastle Island, where, between 1853 and the early 1870s, operations would continually start, cease, and restart.

James Hector of the Palliser Expedition visited Nanaimo in 1860 and examined the coal strata of the area. Two seams of coal were identified on Exit Passage (see Hector's cross-sectional map of Newcastle Island). The Newcastle seam, six feet thick, had been worked to a considerable extent (see Hector's map of the Newcastle mine workings) but was not in operation during Hector's visit, though there were large heaps of coal waiting for a market.[23] Two years after Hector's visit the HBC sold its Nanaimo coal-mining interests to the Vancouver Coal Mining and Land Company. The *British Colonist* of November 10, 1862, proclaimed that the new owners would be more vigorous than had the HBC in developing the mines to their true potential. The new owner immediately contracted out operations at the Newcastle mine site. From 1862 until 1868 John Thompson, Samuel Fiddick, Joseph Bevilockway, Jesse Sage, and Edward Walker were among those contracted to remove coal from this seam.[24] These pioneer settlers had been in Nanaimo since 1854. Thompson, Bevilockway, Sage, and their families arrived from Staffordshire, England, on the first voyage of the *Princess Royal*, which arrived in Nanaimo (via Victoria) on November 27, 1854.[25]

They may not, however, be far removed from this horizon. On the outside of Dodd Narrows stands the Island of Gabriola. It has a length of ten by an average breadth of about three miles, and, judging from an examination across the strike at the North-west end, and along it on the South-west side, the rocks of the island seem to consist almost wholly of brownish-gray sandstone, sometimes becoming conglomerate, particularly on the South-west side. No coal-seams were observed to be associated with the strata.· The dip on the outside of the island appears to be North-eastward, with an average inclination of about four degrees. But in Rocky Bay at the North end, towards the West side, there are evidences of a small undulation.

"The area, including all the coal-seams which have been already mentioned as belonging to the Nanaimo field, has a length from the Dunsmuir claim to the end of Gabriola Island of about sixteen miles, with an average breadth of about six miles. Its surface would then measure upwards of ninety square miles. In the remaining part of this basin, to the South-east, no important coal-seams, as far as I am aware, have as yet been met with. But little of the region is up to the present known, and there is every probability that the same seams will extend to it."

The operations in the Vancouver Coal Company's workings are fully illustrated by the annexed Return:—

VANCOUVER COAL MINE, 1874.

Output of Coal for 12 months ending 31st Dec., 1874.	No. of tons sold for home consumption.	No. of tons sold for exportation.	No. of tons on hand 1st January, 1874.	No. of tons unsold, including coal in stock, 1st Jan. '75.
51,728 4-5th tons.	18,878	32,319		5,065

No. of hands employed.			Wages per day.		
Whites 204	Chinese 61	Indians 19	Whites $1 75 to $3 75	Chinese $1 12½ to $1 25	Indians $1 25 to $1 50

Miners' earnings $2 75 to $5 a day.

Name of Mine, distance from water, &c.	Nanaimo Colliery, situate at Nanaimo Town and at Newcastle Island. At former place, mine is rather over half a mile from wharf; at the latter, say 200 yards.
Value of Plant, Machinery, Railway, and Rolling Stock (not including Workshops, Stores and Dwellings)	$93,657.
Total depth of mines; average thickness of seams	*Douglas Mine,* 450 yards by slope; vertical depth below surface, 400 feet; seam, 4 feet average, perfectly clean. *Chase River Mine* (or seam), 290 feet deep by shaft; seam variable in thickness, 4 to 11 feet, but mixed with shale. *Newcastle Mine,* 240 yards by slope; vertical depth below surface, 90 feet; thickness of seam, 7 to 8 feet, intersected with bands of shale. *Fitzwilliam Mine,* Newcastle Island, 720 yards by slope; vertical depth below surface, 250 feet; thickness of seam (which is interrupted by a fault), 2½ feet to 5½ feet.
Number, horse-power, and kind of Engines at the Mines	On the surface, 1 horizontal pumping and winding engine, 45 horse-power; 1 beam winding and pumping engine, 22 horse-power; 1 horizontal engine, 90 horse-power, in reserve; 2 horizontal engines (coupled), each 10 horse power; 2 locomotives (1 in reserve), 10 and 12 horse-power; 3 steam winches, 5, 8, and 10 horse-power (1 in reserve). *In the Mines,* a 7 in. and a 4½ double-acting steam pump. *In Reserve,* a large patent steam pump, 20 inch steam cylinder, and 6½ inch water cylinder.

(Signed)   M. BATE.

Report of the Minister of Mines for 1874, as presented by Mark Bate for the Vancouver Coal Mining and Land Company. Note: The description given for the Newcastle and Fitzwilliam mines as well as wages and "classes" of those employed is quite interesting.

A square-rigged sailing vessel at anchor in Nanaimo Harbour, waiting to take on a load of coal.

The first report of the provincial minister of mines in 1874 mentioned two mines on Newcastle Island—the Newcastle (with a slope of 240 yards) and the Fitzwilliam (with a slope of 720 yards). By 1876 the Newcastle mine was no longer viable, and, according to that year's report of the provincial minister of mines, its operations ceased. In contrast, the Fitzwilliam mine passed a rock fault in 1875 where miners drove into good five-foot thick coal.

A second wharf was built in Midden Bay to service the Fitzwilliam mine and to assist in the loading of coal barrels. The barque *Wellington* took the first coal shipment from this dock to San Francisco on April 30, 1875. Previous to the opening of the Fitzwilliam mine, the miners working the Newcastle Island coal seams arrived by canoe. From the vicinity of the Bastion they would paddle past the Millstone River delta (then known as Pemberton's Encampment), the "Euclataw Ranch," and north through Exit Channel (Newcastle Island Passage) to the loading dock.[26] With the opening and success of the Fitzwilliam mine, D. W. Gordon was contracted to build miners' houses behind the beach. A photo of this site, taken from Pimbury Point, indicates the magnitude of the settlement that had become established on Newcastle Island.

The relationship between the mine owners and the miners in the Nanaimo coal fields could never be described as harmonious. From the very first, there were concerns over wages and working conditions. These concerns grew into major confrontations that eventually triggered political intervention and the use of the militia. However, by this time Newcastle Island was no longer an active mining site.

Nanaimo mining operations were notorious for loss of life and injury, and those on Newcastle Island were no exception. On June 10, 1874, William Beck was killed when a tunnel collapsed. On 15 September, 1876, three men died in a gas explosion in the Fitzwilliam mine. Of this accident the Coroner's Jury reported: "We find that George Brown, Mathew McDowell and the Chinese Get, came to their deaths from the effects of Black Damp. There was gross negligence on the part of the Officers and Superintendent of the Mine in not having a duly qualified person to examine the mine before any workman was allowed to go down in the morning."[27] The coroner and the jury differed over the verdict, the former feeling that the men were as much to blame as the officials. The jury would not change its verdict, and its report went on record without change. As a result of this accident the Fitzwilliam mine had the dubious distinction of being the first Nanaimo mine in which life was lost due to an explosion.[28]

In 1877 the Fitzwilliam mine employed 40 men underground, utilizing two shifts of 20 men apiece. A year later slackness in the coal market and ongoing problems with ventilation saw the mine close, but pumps kept it de-watered through 1879. Reopened in 1880, it continued production until 1883 when a new shaft, No. 1 Esplanade, was completed on the Nanaimo waterfront, tapping the Douglas seam at 635 feet (193 metres). With the mining focus redirected, the Fitzwilliam closed and coal mining at Midden Bay and Newcastle Island ceased.

Although active mining on Newcastle Island had stopped, the search for new coal deposits and better access to known seams continued. In 1898 the New Vancouver Coal Mining and Land Company began to sink a shaft a short distance inland from Kanaka Bay. Sixty men were assembled to erect the pithead, working triple shifts. A steam engine was also installed, as was a giant fan to provide the desired ventilation. It is also believed that during this period a dam was built, creating Mallard Lake as a water source for steam generation.

Late in the year miners struck the Newcastle seam at 324 feet (98 metres); the following year they struck the Douglas seam at 384 feet (117 metres). With the addition of a 10-foot (3-metre) sump, the total depth for this shaft was 394 feet (120 metres). It was intended that a large area of coal be worked from this location, whose connections to the No. 1 Esplanade and to the Protection Island shaft would have enabled it to be adequately ventilated. Its design also called for the installation of a ladder so that miners could escape in case of an emergency. A year later, however, the idea of this pit-head was shelved. Given the tunnel between Protection Island and No. 1 Esplanade, it was considered quicker to remove the coal being mined under Newcastle via the No. 1 pit-head.

The method of mining under Newcastle Island was known as "pillar and stall." Tunnels were driven into the coal and wider chambers driven off the tunnels (see illustration). This method only succeeded in removing about one-third of the coal; the remainder—known as pillars—was left to support the overhead strata. During this period, miners learned to tell time by the comings and goings of the scheduled steamship services. Each ship had a distinctive rumble to its engines, and this could be distinguished deep in the mines.

At the beginning of the First World War, the Brechin mine across Newcastle Island Passage began operations. Via a tunnel beneath the passage this mine worked both the Douglas and Newcastle coal seams—the same seams on which the Fitzwilliam mine had thrived. Many years later, the idea of using this tunnel as an underground pedestrian access to Newcastle Island was considered but has not yet been developed.

The Newcastle Island shaft remained as an exhaust ventilator for the No. 1 pit-head until 1938, when the mine closed due to a cave-in between it and the Protection Island workings. Coal mining was no longer an active part of Newcastle Island's industrial activities

TODAY

Some of the early coal-working activities on Newcastle Island are still easily observable. A short stiff climb southeast of Saltery Bay will bring you to a flat ramp where the coal cars from the Newcastle mine were pushed to the loading facilities at Midden Bay. Even though an entrance to one of these levels had been dynamited to close it off, up until a few years ago you could squeeze into this mine and venture a fair distance underground. For reasons of public safety this entrance has now been sealed. Walking along this ramp towards Midden Bay the depressions made by, and the foundations of, some early buildings are still visible.

Evidence of the Fitzwilliam mine is not so easily detected. In the southwest corner of Midden Bay loose slabs of sandstone projecting out into the bay indicate the original approach to one of the wharves. Behind this sandstone protuberance, large depressions in front of the cliff indicate the location of the old mine entrance. Along the beach and in the eroding banks, red firecracked rock, clinkers, ash, and coal fragments offer century-old evidence of the Newcastle and Fitzwilliam mines.

Inland from Kanaka Bay, just west of where the Kanaka Bay Trail turns south towards the Canadian Pacific Railway Pavilion, is the 1898-1900 construction site of the New Vancouver Coal Mining and Land Company's ventilation shaft. The concrete pad and part of the exhaust flue are still in place. At one time it was possible to descend nearly 400 feet by ladder and follow the mine workings all the way to downtown Nanaimo—a straight-line distance of 4.5 kilometres or 2.8 miles!

COAL COMPANY CHRONOLOGY AND OWNERSHIP OF THE NANAIMO COAL FIELDS

1853 The HBC forms the Nanaimo Coal Company, which operates its mines until 1862.

1862 The HBC sells all its coal-mining interests to the Vancouver Coal Mining and Land Company, a British corporation.

1889 The Vancouver Coal Mining and Land Company becomes the New Vancouver Coal Mining and Land Company.

1902 The New Vancouver Coal Mining and Land Company is sold to the Western Fuel Company of San Francisco.

1918 The Western Fuel Company is reorganized as the Canadian Western Fuel Company.

1928 The Canadian Western Fuel Company is bought out by Canadian Collieries (Dunsmuir) Limited.

1982 The mineral rights under Newcastle Island are acquired by the Crown.

PROPERTIES OF NEWCASTLE ISLAND SANDSTONE

According to a 1917 report on Canadian building materials, the Newcastle quarry was unique: "This stone differs strikingly in general appearance from any other sandstone tested. It is of fine and even grain, with true light-grey colour and clean 'pepper and salt' appearance. Smooth surfaces present a fine-dotted aspect, with light coloured grains in excess of the scattered greenish-grey specks." The light grains are orthoclase and plagioclase feldspars and quartz; the dark grains are biotite mica. "Hardness is undoubtedly the most troublesome property of this stone, and its lighter colour compared to other sandstones in the Gulf Islands, its chief advantage."[29]

Physical Properties:

Specific gravity weight per cubic foot = 152.38 pounds

Pore space = 8.15 per cent

Crushing strength when dry = 14,849 pounds per square inch; when wet = 11,874 pounds/square inch; when frozen = 9,670 pounds/square inch

Chemical Composition:

Insoluble material = 94.09 per cent

Soluble material = 5.91 per cent

Analysis of Soluble Material:

Alumina = 2.02 per cent

Ferric oxide = .04 per cent

Ferrous oxide = 1.43 per cent

Lime = .63 per cent

Magnesia = .55 per cent

Carbonic acid = .05 per cent

CHAPTER 5

THE ROLE OF SANDSTONE

As a by-product of their early coal-mining activity, the HBC and its employees were well aware that quality building stone, in the form of a hard durable sandstone, was present in large quantities in the Nanaimo area.[30] The HBC first removed small amounts of this stone to build fireplaces in its Victoria offices. However, it was James Hector's Palliser Expedition report of 1860 that formally noted the flawless nature, unusual strength, and weather-resistant properties of Newcastle sandstone. It was another decade before the importance of these qualities gained formal recognition.

On the basis of Hector's report, in the summer of 1869 Joseph Emery, contractor for the new United States Mint in San Francisco, visited Nanaimo to inspect the sandstone. Later in October, in company with Mark Bate

ARABELLA MAY BATE GILLESPIE OWEN 1893-1984

Arabella was born in Cumberland, British Columbia, a granddaughter of Mark Bate, Nanaimo's first mayor. It was Mark Bate who, as manager of the Vancouver Coal Mining and Land Company, signed the contract that permitted the quarrying of sandstone for the construction of the U.S. Mint in San Francisco. Arabella's first husband, Andrew Gillespie, died in Seattle in 1935. She married Ernest Owen, of Arizona, in 1939.

Later, as a resident of San Francisco, Arabella contributed the story of the Newcastle Island "sandstone contract" to the California Historical Society. Later, she was one of the people instrumental in having the mint declared a National Historic Site.

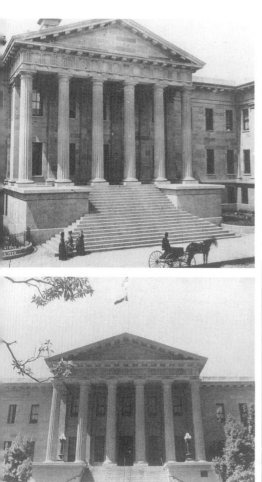

THE UNITED STATES MINT: SAN FRANCISCO

Considered one of the finest examples of American Federal Classic Revival Architecture, the "Old Mint" was the first building of this style to be constructed in the United States. It was designed by Alfred B. Mullett, supervising architect of the United States Treasury. Land for the mint was purchased in 1867 at a cost of $100,000 in gold coin. Construction began on April 1, 1869; the cornerstone was laid on May 25, 1870; and the finished building was turned over to the government on November 6, 1874. Cost of construction was $2,130,512.

In keeping with its purpose, the mint was of exceedingly solid construction. The building was constructed of brick and faced with 12-inch-thick sandstone. Metal shutters, ornamental iron stair railings, granite floors, and Honduran mahogany woodwork completed the interior design.

The *San Francisco Call* of November 1, 1874, described this impressive building in glowing terms: "The fire department will have little trouble quenching any conflagration that may rise within its walls, and unless an earthquake gives it a subterranean quietus, it bids fair to stand up for centuries." The endurance test came on the morning of April 18, 1906, when the great San Francisco earthquake struck. Virtually the whole city was destroyed—either by the quake and its aftershocks or by the great fire that followed. The intensity of the heat from burning structures around the mint actually melted some glass in its windows, but the interior remained undamaged. After the fire, the mint was the only financial institution in San Francisco that was able to carry on business.

In 1934, one-third of the entire US gold reserve was stored in the San Franscico mint. It continued in operation until 1937, when paper money began to replace coin as legal tender. In 1961 the building was declared a national landmark and, by order of President Richard Nixon, on March 23, 1972, it was spared demolition. Up to 1994 it functioned, in part, as a numismatic museum. Today, this still-impressive building remains on the corner of Fifth and Mission Street. With nearly 8,000 tons of Newcastle Island sandstone having gone into its construction, the building remains well worth a visit.

(Left) The United States Mint, San Francisco, in its late construction phase. Note the two rough Newcastle sandstone columns near the centre of the photograph. Portico of the United States Mint, San Francisco late nineteenth century (top left). "The Old Mint" after its restoration in 1976 (middle left). Front of US Mint, 1982 (top right). US Mint, south side, 1982 (middle right).

(manager of the Vancouver Coal Mining and Land Company and, later, the first mayor of Nanaimo) and Mr. Stebbins (superintendent for the mint), Emery returned to Nanaimo. Finding the Newcastle stone superior to anything else they had seen, Emory signed a five-year agreement with the Vancouver Coal Mining and Land Company to cut stone. The selection of Newcastle stone for such a prestigious building as the San Francisco mint aroused considerable jealousy and prejudice, especially on the part of quarries in the western United States. Consequently, the Newcastle stone was subjected to severe testing. In all instances, it proved to be of superior quality.

Forty men were hired that winter to prepare the site, to construct buildings, and to secure the equipment to begin operation. Their small settlement beside Newcastle Island Passage was called Perriman. The local proprietor was J. G. Dawes, and his quarry manager was Richard Nightingale. In the spring of 1870 the first of the three-masted sailing schooners arrived at the new quarry wharf and soon carried to San Francisco the first of the 8,000 tons of sandstone destined for the construction of the mint. At this time the quarry crew numbered 50 workers, with the expectation of being augmented by an additional 37 Chinese from San Francisco. The price of sandstone was three dollars per ton. Large blocks brought double this amount.

The contract included six blank cylinders that would be sculpted into monolithic Doric columns to support the mint's portico. The finished design featured columns 27 feet 6 inches long and 3 feet 10 inches in

The construction of the British Columbia Penitentiary (1876 to 1878) required many tons of sandstone from the Newcastle Island quarry.

The original Alexandria Suspension Bridge that allowed the Cariboo Wagon Road to cross the Fraser River near Spuzzum, BC. Sandstone from Newcastle was used in the construction of its supports. Notice the road winding along the hillside to the right of the river on the upper photo. The lower two pictures show the bridge today.

diameter. The Newcastle quarry produced eight of the 30-ton blanks, two of which were on the ill-fated *Zephyr* when it sank off Mayne Island in February 1872 (see Chapter 6).

Emory's lease expired in 1875. Kinsman and Styles, builders and contractors from Victoria, then leased the quarry to remove 2,000 tons of stone to be used in the building of the British Columbia Penitentiary, which was to be located near New Westminster. Over the next 80 years a succession of companies and leases continued to extract Newcastle building stone for many prominent buildings in Nanaimo, Vancouver, Victoria, Seattle, and San Francisco. This stone was even used in the construction of a mausoleum in Napa, California! Newspaper reports indicate that a number of sandstone blocks were quarried in 1872 to be used in the construction of the Alexandria Suspension Bridge. This bridge was an important part of the Cariboo Wagon Road, which crosses the Fraser Canyon near Spuzzum (between Yale and Boston Bar). As this bridge was built in 1863, any Newcastle sandstone appears to have been used to raise the bridge. On a recent visit to the old bridge site I noted that sandstone had indeed been used and that it appeared to be from Newcastle. Archival records of contracts issued for public works contain a number of gaps and are inconclusive with regard to this issue.

Once the quarry was fully operational and the working face prepared, single blocks of stone up to 50 feet long could be cut. A series of holes were drilled in a line, then widened in the direction of the desired break (see sketch). Charges were placed in each hole and exploded

WEDGES, FEATHERS, AND IRONS

The most time-consuming job of the Newcastle quarrymen was cutting and shaping the sandstone blocks to the required dimensions. This was often done with hand tools. Even today, inspection of the leavings indicates the process they used. First, a series of finger-deep holes was drilled into the stone along the plane of the desired split. Into these holes feathers were placed, and between the feathers a wedge. By pounding the wedges down between the feathers evenly, the rock could be split (depending on its bedding plane) in a fairly straight line. Before steam-powered drilling machines, the manual drilling of these "finger" holes was very tedious. Inside the sandstone quarry the types of drill holes used to "free," shape, and dress the stone are still visible.

Working and shaping sandstone. Left and bottom: The Wedge and Feather method of cutting sandstone blocks into the desired dimensions. Top right: The way in which the long drill holes were widened to break off large blocks. Centre: An illustration of the JB monogram one of the workers etched into the quarry wall. This can still be seen today!

simultaneously, breaking the giant slab free. Using wedges and feathers (see insert) as well as hand tools, these slabs were cut or shaped to produce whatever size blocks were required. Great amounts of rubble were also produced. This material was very suitable for masonry work but, as there was little demand for this type of stone, it was usually dumped nearby. Piles of this unwanted rubble are still visible along the shore of Newcastle Island Passage. Some of it was scavenged for use in the construction of the Hirst warehouse in 1874. The Hirst building is now part of the Harbour Commission Offices on Front Street,[31] but the stone used from the Newcastle quarry, having been plastered and painted over, is no longer visible.

Perriman saw many crew changes during its heyday, as various companies settled in for periods of time that were dependent on the size of their respective contracts. In the 1920s the McDonald Cut-Stone Company leased the quarry. Also photos from the Peter Schwartz collection

Christ Church Cathedral, Victoria, opened in 1926.

LESSEES OF NEWCASTLE ISLAND'S SANDSTONE QUARRY

Year	Company	Location	Building
1870	Joseph Emery of San Francisco	San Francisco	United States Mint
1872	Joseph Emery	near Spuzzum, BC	Alexandria Bridge
1875	Kinsman & Styles of Victoria, BC	New Westminster	BC Penitentiary
1879	Kinsman & Styles of Victoria, BC	Victoria	Odd Fellows Hall
1880	Robertson & Co.	Victoria	Esquimalt Graving Dock
1890	Newcastle Island Quarry Company	Seattle	W. Marshal Building Post & Edwards Building
1892	Carter & Nightingale	Vancouver	Bank of Montreal Bank of British North America
1904		Napa California	Private Mausoleum
1907	Northwest Construction Co. of Oakland, CA	San Francisco	San Francisco Dry Dock
		Vancouver Vancouver	Lord Nelson School BC Permanent Loan Co. Building
1908	Newcastle Quarry Company of Tacoma Washington	Victoria	St. John Church
1927	McDonald Cut-Stone Company	Victoria	Christ Church (Anglican) Cathedral
1955		Victoria	Christ Church (Anglican)

Charlie Roberts, Quarry Manager, McDonald Cut-Stone Company Quarry. The cutting machine can be seen in the top left corner.

Clem Cuthbert and George Donahue, foreman finishing a pulpstone on the lathe in the McDonald Cut-Stone Company Quarry, c. 1925.

document stone being cut for Christ Church Cathedral in Victoria. The last stone was removed in 1955 and was used for an addition to the church. Bob Spearing, now a resident of Victoria, remembers this as the toughest half-day's work he had ever done. Hungarian stone cutters (who lived in tents) had cut the stone, and Bob's job was to wheel it down a muddy hill, across a shaky landing, and onto a waiting scow (Bob Sperling, personal communication).

In 1973, with President Richard Nixon's re-dedication of San Francisco's old mint, the US Federal Reserve contractor requested 1,000 cubic feet of Newcastle sandstone for restoration work. This request was turned down by BC Parks in 1974 for environmental reasons. Of the many sandstone quarry sites in British Columbia's Gulf Islands, none is believed to have produced better stone than the Perriman site on Newcastle Island.

PULP-STONES: THE MCDONALD CUT-STONE COMPANY

In 1923 a new industry was established along Newcastle Island Passage. One mile south of the sandstone quarry, Messrs J. A. and C. H. McDonald formed the McDonald Cut-Stone Company to cut cylindrical sandstone blocks. These blocks would grind wood into pulp in preparation for paper-making. The McDonalds employed as many as 20 men, including George Donahue who, as quarry foreman, made $10 per day. Nick Gerolin, the steam engineer, made $6 per day; Charlie Roberts, the certified blaster, made $5 per day; and the labourers made $4 per day (Arabella May Owen, personal communication).

A large cutting machine was built that would cut a 54-inch-in-diameter cylinder of stone to a depth of approximately 40 inches. Steel shot, heated white hot then quenched in cold water to "split," was used as the cutting agent. When the cut was completed—a noisy process that took about 45 minutes—a horizontal hole was drilled at the base. A small charge of black powder, placed in this hole, was detonated to break the stone free. Giant tongs and a derrick were then used to lift the stone to a large lathe, where it was trimmed to the required dimensions. Newcastle stones, when finished, were about 48 inches in diameter and 18 to 20 inches high. The McDonalds left no samples of their work, but one donated symbol of that era remains. The finished stone beside the Newcastle quarry came from Gabriola Island, courtesy of Clive Coates. The Gabriola pulp-stones had slightly different dimensions than those on Newcastle Island, being 56 by 20 inches (142 by 51 centimetres) when finished. Once finished, these stones were shipped to pulp mills along the Pacific coast, including those at Port Alberni and Powell River. Their lifespan in the pulp-making process lasted from three to 20 months.

In 1932 the Newcastle Island operation was relocated to Gabriola Island, where it remained until new technology won out. The production of pulp-stones in British Columbia ceased when artificial stones, with a lifespan of four to five years, began to be manufactured.

Nanaimo Free Press

LOCAL QUARRY WILL SUPPLY BIG PILLARS

Pillars for B.C. Permanent Building in Vancouver will be Highest in British Columbia

The Northwestern Construction Company, who have control of the stone quarry on Newcastle Island, have received a contract for a big order. It is for the getting out of pillars for the B.C. Permanent building being constructed in Vancouver. The pillars will be 36 feet high and the pattern which the company received last night was for solid stone blocks for these pillars, 16 feet in height. When the pillars are completed they will be the highest pillars in any building in British Columbia.

The excerpt (left) from the October 24, 1907, Nanaimo Free Press *refers to the building that still stands in the 300 block West Pender in Vancouver. Recently recognized for its place in Vancouver architectural history, the Newcastle pillars are featured in* Postcards from the Past: Edwardian Images of Greater Vancouver and the Fraser Valley. *This book won the 1997 City of Vancouver Heritage Award. Authors Fred Thirkell and Robert Scullion describe the building as follows: "On the south side of the street stands an architectural gem, a small 'temple bank' in Beaux-Arts, Neo-Classical style, designed by Hooper and Watkinson in 1907 for the BC Permanent Loan Company. The building retains some of the city's finest Tiffany-style stained glass as well as outstanding architectural detailing."*

The S.S. Lakme *at the sandstone quarry about to load stone. c. 1896. Note: In the background sits a forested Brechin Point, now the site of the Brechin Point Marine and Petro Canada Bulk Fuel Unloading Facility.*

"THE LADIES FROM FRASER STREET"

Wages for pulp-stone cutting were better than average in the late 1920s and, as most of the workers were single, they lived quite well. Little wonder that a fair percentage of their take-home pay went into various watering holes around Nanaimo and/or into the palms of "ladies of the evening." One highly acclaimed "house" was located on Fraser Street. "With free time on their hands," a few of the ladies from this house decided to pay their quarry friends a day visit. They hired a boat to take them across the channel to Newcastle Island, whereupon their arrival quickly became a "special occasion." It was reported that even the hard-driving quarry foreman, George Donahue, called "lunch" a bit early this day (Arabella May Owen, personal communication).

MYTHS OF STONE

Over the years a number of erroneous stories have evolved, declaring Newcastle Island to be the source of stone for public buildings both in Nanaimo and Vancouver. To correct some of these stories, here is a list of those buildings that used sandstone taken from quarries other than the one on Newcastle Island.

Building	Quarry
Nanaimo Courthouse[32]	Protection Island Quarry
Nanaimo Post Office Original building 1883	Machine Shop Quarry
1911 addition and tower (1912)	Jack Point Quarry
Vancouver, Carnegie Library	Gabriola Island Quarry
Victoria, Carnegie Library	Saturna Island, Taylor's Point Quarry

The old Nanaimo Post Office (now demolished) was built in 1883 with sandstone from the Machine Shop Quarry' in Nanaimo, not from Newcastle Island.

The sandstone quarry as it was in operation, May 22, 1926 (upper left). The crane and pulley systems were used to lift and move the sandstone blocks. It is believed that the stone being quarried was for use in the construction of the Anglican Christ Church Cathedral in Victoria (under construction above). The quarry face, May 22, 1926 (middle right). The worker is preparing a block of stone for splitting with wedges and feathers, some in place. The cutting machine (middle left) used at the quarry to cut the cylindrical blanks. The cutter is the large cylinder seen projecting slightly from the left of the housing. The machine was moved on a small dolly on rails. Pulp-stones (bottom) finished and awaiting shipment. Notice the method of inserting the tongs for lifting.

THE *ZEPHYR*: ITS "SPECS"

Built: 1855 in Medford, Massachusets, for Lombard & Co. of Boston

Length: approximately 125 feet (estimated between 100 to 150 feet) Breadth: 25 to 30 feet

Draft: 13 feet

Weight: 415 tons

Rigging: As a three-masted barque (forward and main mast, square rigged; mizzen mast, rigged fore and aft)

After spending its early years in the east coast trade and in trans-Atlantic commerce, the *Zephyr* was purchased by a group of San Francisco businessmen and brought to the west coast in 1860. The *British Colonist*'s "Shipping News" reports the *Zephyr*'s first arrival in British Columbia in 1865 and offers subsequent accounts of its voyages. An event of interest to Nanaimo occurred in October 1871. The *Zephyr*, under the command of Captain Small, slipped out of Nanaimo Harbour to avoid the service of a writ concerning default on a consignment of lumber.[33]

CHAPTER 6

TREASURE FROM THE ZEPHYR

On January 31, 1872, Victoria's *British Colonist* reported that the barque *Zephyr* had arrived at the sandstone quarry on Newcastle Island to take on a load of stone destined for the US mint in San Francisco.[34] The *Zephyr* was one of a number of vessels chartered to transport the 8,000 tons of sandstone required for the mint's construction. Far from unique, the *Zephyr* was but one of hundreds of similar vessels that regularly added their masts to the floating forest of square-riggers at the wharves in Victoria, New Westminster, and Nanaimo.

At Newcastle it took quarry labourers and the *Zephyr*'s crew 11 days to load an estimated 800 tons of stone. Included were two grand 27.5-foot-long, 46-inch-in-diameter cylinders. These 33-ton columns were intended for the mint's portico and were carefully loaded along with over 120 72-cubic-foot stone blocks that weighed 5.5 tons apiece. At 10:00 a.m. on February 12, 1872, the *Zephyr* cleared Departure Bay. The weather was not good, and all on board prepared themselves for a rough passage south through the Straits of Georgia and Juan de Fuca to the open Pacific.

Moving southeast, the crew fought a headwind as the night sky darkened. About 8:00 p.m. the wind veered to northwest, driving a blinding snowstorm before it. Despite a double lookout, the watch found it

---

WHAT IS A ZEPHYR?

Zephyrus (Latin) or Zephyros (Greek) was the god of the west wind. As used today, zephyr refers to a gentle breeze or a breeze from the west.

WRECK AT MAYNE ISLAND—TWO LIVES LOST

Intelligence reached the U.S. Consul on Monday evening that the American bark *Zephyr*, stone-laden for San Francisco had been totally lost near Mayne Island and the Captain (Hepson) and a seaman named James Stewart were drowned. The news was brought by the chief officer (Mr. Lusk) and all but two of the survivors of the crew. The *Zephyr* sailed from Newcastle for San Francisco with stone for the new Mint on Monday last. On the following morning, at 3½ o'clock, during a blinding snow-storm, she struck on the low, rocky shore of Mayne Island, knocking a great hole in her bilge. The vessel began to sink rapidly and at 6½ o'clock turned on her side and went down in 90 feet of water. All hands—save Captain Hepson, Stewart, and the cook—succeeded in reaching the boat, and getting clear of the wreck. The boat lay alongside until daybreak, when the cook was discovered clinging to the foreyard and was rescued. Search was made for the missing men, but they had sunk to rise no more. The crew experienced much difficulty in reaching this port, owing to the high wind that prevailed for several days. They are in a destitute condition, having saved none of their effects, and are kindly cared for by Consul Eckstien. The second mate and one man remain to watch; but no hope is entertained of saving her. The mainmast is about 20 feet out of water at low tide.

This report of the loss of the Zephyr *appeared in the* British Colonist *newspaper, February 20, 1872.*

Two entries in Victoria's Colonist *newspaper on January 31, 1872, indicated the ship's arrival in Nanaimo. "The bark* Zephyr, *sixty-two days from San Pedro, California arrived in Nanaimo on Monday evening. She was given up for lost." The 62-day journey was considered a very long time for this passage. A second note said: "The bark* Zephyr *and the brig* Orient *arrived at the Stone Quarry, Nanaimo, yesterday. The* Zephyr *was towed into Departure Bay by the* Otter." *Here (upper left) the* Otter *is seen in Nanaimo's harbour years later.*

Three-masted, square-rigged sailing vessels at anchor. These vessels, very similar to the Zephyr, *were the workhorses of maritime trading in the late nineteenth century.*

impossible to distinguish land from sea. Early the following morning, hearing breakers and fearful that they were on a lee shore, Captain Hepson tried to wear the ship off. He lacked the sea room to do so and, as a last resort, he ordered the bow anchor dropped. The anchor failed to hold, and the heavy seas gradually pushed the *Zephyr* against Mayne Island. In

A plaque on Newcastle today commemorates the loss of the Zephyr. *Below is the Bastion in earlier years.*

the words of the survivors, it then "began to pound heavily." Fearing the it would sink, Hepson ordered his crew to "clew up the sails" and prepare to leave the vessel at first light. There was no panic, and the *Zephyr* remained on an even keel and out of immediate danger.

History shows that, around 5:00 a.m., the heavy cargo of sandstone shifted, causing the ship's port rail to heel under. Terrified, the men scrambled for safety. Six of the crew got a lifeboat clear of the wallowing *Zephyr*. Two sailors were swept overboard. Hepson apparently went below decks to find James Stewart, the remaining crewman.

The lifeboat stayed by the wreck until morning, where the survivors located the cook clinging to the foreyard. Later they made their way ashore, where they found one of the missing seamen alive but in poor condition. That afternoon all eight survivors made their way overland to Active Pass, where they took refuge in a fisher's cabin.

The next morning the *Zephyr*'s first mate, Mr. Lusk; two of the crew; and the fisher returned to the *Zephyr*. Only its royal mast and top gallants showed above water. No trace could be found of Hepson or Stewart.

News of the wreck appeared in the *British Colonist* of February 20, 1872. Before departing for San Francisco, the crew made a deposition to a Victoria notary, Robert Bishop. A few weeks later, the *Colonist* reported that C. T. Millard had attended an auction and paid $4,250 for the *Zephyr*'s salvage right. There is no record of attempts at salvage. The *Zephyr* settled to the bottom for a long rest—a rest not to be interrupted for more than a century.

THE *ZEPHYR* REBORN

After 104 years of obscurity, the wreck of the *Zephyr* gained new attention when, in 1976, Gary LeTour of Mayne Island and the Underwater Archaeological Society of British Columbia (UASBC) initiated searches. After several months, Gary located the remains of the *Zephyr* between Edith Point and David's Cove, south of Active Pass on the east side of Mayne Island. The wreck lay in 6 to 7 fathoms (36 to 42 feet or 11 to 13 metres) of water. Gary and the UASBC then undertook a joint survey. During this survey it soon became apparent that the *Zephyr* was an important time capsule, containing much information regarding early west coast shipping. At the urging of the UASBC, the provincial government designated the *Zephyr* a "protected site" under the Provincial Heritage Conservation Act.

Prominent among the visible portions of the wreck were the two sandstone columns and a "mountain" of the cut stone blocks. During reconnaissance and early excavation, a number of artefacts were raised, including the *Zephyr*'s chronometer and sextant, some china, cutlery, and even crystal doorknobs! Lacking a facility in which to preserve, store, and, more important, display these artefacts, further excavation was postponed.

In November 1984 the UASBC prepared a proposal that identified Newcastle Island Provincial Park as a desirable and appropriate location for an exhibit focusing on the *Zephyr*. The *Zephyr*, this proposal contended, was "Newcastle Island's ship." The resources required to undertake the UASBC proposal, however, were not available. A major component of the proposal called for the raising of the sandstone columns and some of the cut block cargo. This material was to appear in displays at Newcastle Island, Maffeo Sutton Park, the Mayne Island Museum, and the Maritime Museum in Vancouver. Early in 1987, David Griffiths, UASBC president, was able to secure the requisite $22,000 from the Provincial Ministry of Environment and Parks and the Nanaimo Harbour Commission.

By October, under the direction of Gary Bridges of the UASBC, the logistics were completed. On the morning of October 14 the 200-ton-capacity floating derrick *McKenzie* from the Fraser River Pile and Dredge Company was moved into position over the wreck site. During the day the two columns and five 5.5-ton sandstone blocks were successfully raised, and the next day the *McKenzie* was in Newcastle Island Passage ready to discharge one of the former. With what seemed like scarcely any effort at all one of the 33-ton columns was placed ashore. After an absence of 115 years and 245 days, this column was back to within a few metres of where it was quarried. All present hastily climbed aboard the landed cylinder for a photo opportunity. Then the *McKenzie* was off to Vancouver. What a century before had taken days had

THE UNDERWATER ARCHAEOLOGICAL SOCIETY OF BRITISH COLUMBIA

The UASBC became a registered non-profit society in 1975. Its aims are to "study, protect, preserve and present the historic resources of British Columbia's coastal waters."

The *Zephyr* is but one of a number of shipwreck projects with which the UASBC has been involved. The "*Zephyr* Project" was headed by David Griffiths, the society's president; Gary Bridges, vice-president; and Tom Beasley. The assistance of the Fraser River Pile and Dredge Company was of immense importance to the completion of this project.

been accomplished in half an hour. What would those men who had loaded this column on board the *Zephyr* have thought could they have seen this unloading operation?

The *Zephyr* may not have been unique, as sailing vessels went, but with respect to the history of Newcastle Island, our knowledge of BC maritime commerce, and the days of square-rigged sailing ships, it is certainly very special.

CHAPTER 7

KAKUA THE KANAKA

"Horrible if true" was the rumour that spread around Victoria on the night of December 10, 1868. It was believed that a fearful tragedy had occurred in Nanaimo. The next day the *British Colonist* told its readers that, in a fit of jealousy, a Kanaka had killed a number of people.

The Kanakas, early immigrants of Hawaiian descent, have an important place in BC history. Their contribution has been documented in Tom Koppel's *Kanaka*.[35] Of the many Kanakas who arrived on Vancouver Island, Peter Kakua was perhaps the most infamous. Peter joined the services of the HBC in 1853 and worked at various company posts, including those at Fort Vancouver (now Vancouver, Washington), Victoria, and Fort Rupert. He claimed that while in Victoria he served Sir James Douglas personally. Peter eventually arrived in Nanaimo, where he worked for the Vancouver Coal Mining and Land Company and lived with a First Nations woman, Que-en, also known as Mary. By 1868 they had a daughter.

WHO WERE THE KANAKAS?

Kanaka is a collective name given to Native peoples from the South Pacific Islands—in particular, those from the Hawaiian or Sandwich Islands. In the Hawaiian language Kanaka means "person" or "human being."

With the arrival of the North West Company and the Hudson's Bay Company (the latter had a trading post in Hawaii) to coastal British Columbia, Kanakas became a major component of company workforces. Once their term of employment was completed, these individuals were free to follow their own destinies. Some returned to their place of origin, while others remained in British Columbia. Place names such as Kanaka Creek, Kanaka Bar, and Kanaka Bay commemorate their presence in British Columbia.

On the morning of December 4, 1868, several bodies were found in Peter's house. Peter was missing. Special Constable Ashdown Green was directed to accompany Charles Chautrel, Moses Mahaffy, and two First Nations people to search for Peter Kakua. On Newcastle Island they located a fire, with Peter and Stepheny ("a coloured man") sitting beside it. When the group surrounded the two men, Kakua bounded towards the woods, but he fell over a boulder and was easily captured. On the short boat trip back to Nanaimo, Peter worked his hands free and plunged overboard. He attempted to overturn the canoe but was smacked with a paddle, recaptured, and finally lodged in the Nanaimo gaol. Stepheny made no attempt to escape.

An inquest was held in Nanaimo on December 7, 1868, before Police Magistrate Warner Spalding and a 12-man jury headed by Thomas Parker. Pe-

BRITISH COLONIST

DECEMBER 11, 1868

Horrible If True—A rumour prevailed in town last night of a fearful tragedy having been enacted in Nanaimo. A Kanaka is said to have killed his wife, his wife's sister and three children in a fit of jealousy.

DECEMBER 18, 1868

A Kanaka, the alleged perpetrator of the series of shocking murders in Nanaimo, ten days ago, was brought down on the steamer Sir James Douglas yesterday, and committed to prison to await the Assizes.

MARCH 6TH, 1869

Kakue, the Kanaka, will be hanged at Nanaimo on Friday next. He will be sent up on the Sir James Douglas on Tuesday. The executioner (a convict, who receives a pardon for his services) that officiated yesterday will hang Kakuae.

ter's confession provided the sordid details of a multiple murder. He testified that Mary had left him and, via her brother, had sent a message that she no longer intended to live with him. Peter set off on a drinking spree that continued until the afternoon of December 3, when he returned home with the intention of going to bed. However, he found his wife, child, mother-in-law (Squash-e-lek), and father-in-law (Shil-at-ti-nord) sitting around a fire. They indicated that they were there to pack Mary's things. Further enraged, Peter left looking for whisky.

He testified that he returned home again about 2:00 a.m. and found his father-in-law in bed with Mary. A fight ensued, and Mary and Squash-e-lek joined in beating Peter. Angry and intoxicated, Peter claimed that he grabbed an axe and flailed about indiscriminately until he collapsed in

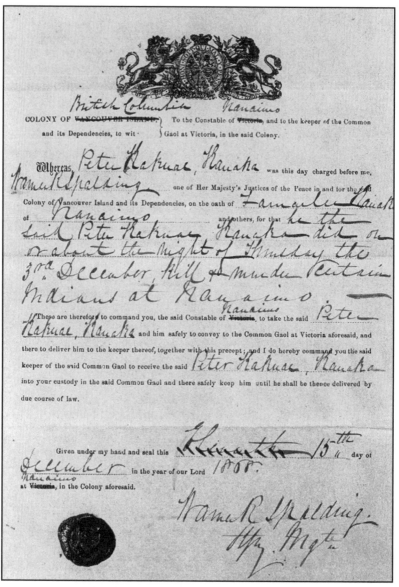

British Columbia — Nanaimo

COLONY OF ~~VANCOUVER ISLAND~~ To the Constable of ~~Victoria~~, and to the keeper of the Common and its Dependencies, to wit · Gaol at Victoria, in the said Colony.

Whereas *Peter Kakua, Kanaka* was this day charged before me, *Warner R Spalding* one of Her Majesty's Justices of the Peace in and for the said Colony of Vancouver Island and its Dependencies, on the oath of *Tamaqula Kanaka* of *Nanaimo* and others, for that *he the said Peter Kakua Kanaka did on or about the night of Thursday the 3rd December, kill & murder certain Indians at Nanaimo.*

These are therefore to command you, the said Constable of ~~Victoria~~ Nanaimo, to take the said *Peter Kakua, Kanaka* and him safely to convey to the Common Gaol at Victoria aforesaid, and there to deliver him to the keeper thereof, together with this precept; and I do hereby command you the said keeper of the said Common Gaol to receive the said *Peter Kakua, Kanaka* into your custody in the said Common Gaol and there safely keep him until he shall be thence delivered by due course of law.

Given under my hand and seal this *Fifteenth 15-th* day of *December* in the year of our Lord *1868.* at ~~Victoria~~ Nanaimo, in the Colony aforesaid.

Warner R Spalding.

The document (above) that transferred Peter Kakua from Nanaimo to stand trial in Victoria was signed by Warner Spalding, the local magistrate. The Supreme Court of British Columbia document (top right) committed Peter Kakua to trial in Victoria in February 1869. This early photo of the Bastion (right) was how it must have looked about the time Peter Kakua was incarcerated. Were these cannons functional? Note the centre bore of the lower middle left muzzle.

In the Supreme Court of Civil Justice of British Columbia.

Regina
versus
Peter Kakue

Victoria, by the Grace of God of the United Kingdom of Great Britain and Ireland, and of the Colonies thereunto belonging, Queen Defender of the Faith.

To *Kaulebehelee.*

Greeting.

WE command you and every of you that, all business being laid aside, and all excuses ceasing, you do in your proper persons appear before The Honorable *Joseph Needham Chief Justice* Matthew Baillie Begbie, Judge of Our Supreme Court of Civil Justice of British *at Victoria* Columbia, assigned to keep Our peace in the said Colony, and also to hear and determine all felonies, trespasses, and other misdemeanors, in Our said Colony, committed at a General Court of Assize to be holden at *Victoria* in and for the said Colony, on *Tuesday* the *18th* day of *February*, now next ensuing, at the hour of *10* in the forenoon of the same day, to testify the truth and give evidence on Our behalf against

,

and attend the Court from day to day until you shall be discharged by the Judge thereof; and this you and every of you are in nowise to omit, under the penalty for you and every of you in such case made and provided.

Herein fail not at your peril.

Dated 15 February 1869.

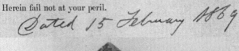

THE HAWAIIAN MEANING
OF THE NAME KAKUA

In the press of the day (1868-69) and the court documents issued for the trial, Peter's surname receives a number of different spellings, including Kakuan, Kakue, and Kakuae. The *Hawaiian Dictionary* gives two meanings for kakua: to bind or fasten, as one would fasten a sarong or belt; an appeal to the gods, usually accompanied by an offering of food.[36]

exhaustion. When he awoke, he found that his child, Mary, and Mary's parents were dead. Peter locked the door and left. Finally, he went to the house of another Kanaka, Famalee, and told him what he had done. Later, again drunk and in the company of Stepheny (who was also considerably intoxicated), Peter went to his canoe, which was hidden under a wharf. Peter wanted to escape to the Mainland but Stepheny would not go, so instead they went ashore on Newcastle Island. Peter concluded his testimony with: "This is all I have to say."

Other witnesses were called. A neighbour, Robert Hughes, testified to being awakened by screaming in the vicinity of Peter's house. Famalee recalled that Peter came to his house and said that he had killed his wife, child, and in-laws. Peter then held up his hand and showed Famalee where his father-in-law had bitten off one of his fingers in the struggle. As Peter was drunk, Famalee did not believe him. Later, however, with Charles York, Famalee went to Peter's house, viewed the bodies, and reported what he had seen to Constable Stewart.

Stepheny testified that Peter put ashore on Newcastle Island and that they drank all day until captured.

Dr. Klein Grant examined the bodies and stated that Peter's father-in-law had his skull cleft, a wound on the right side of his chest, and a hole in his abdomen, from which his intestines protruded. His mother-in-law had a deep cut in the back of her neck; his wife's jugular had been severed; and the child had been almost decapitated.

On December 15 Peter Kakua was formally charged before Police Magistrate Warner R. Spalding with "kill[ing] and slay[ing] certain Indians at Nanaimo." Peter was then shipped to Victoria for trial, arriving December 17 aboard the steamer *Sir James Douglas*. He was committed to prison until the spring assizes.

Peter's formal trial was held in the court house at James Bay, Victoria, on February 10, 1869, before Chief Justice Joseph Needham. It is of interest that the name of British Columbia's legendary "hanging judge,"

Matthew Baillie Begbie, had been scratched out on the Supreme Court document. The attorney-general appeared for the Prosecution. Mr. Ring and Mr. Robertson, instructed by Mr. Bishop, appeared on Peter's behalf. Peter pleaded not guilty.[37]

Two separate trials were held, each on two counts of murder, and the proceedings were covered by the *British Colonist*. Peter was found guilty of the murders, but the jury first recommended mercy on the grounds that, being a Kanaka, he did not "possess the sense of character of his crime as would make the extreme penalty of the law advisable." The second jury showed less mercy. On February 19, 1869, Peter was sentenced to be hanged.

Records in the provincial archives show that the Jurors for Our Lady the Queen found "that Peter Kakue [sic], not having the fear of God before his eyes, but being moved and seduced by the visitation of the devil, on the 4th day of December 1868, feloniously, wilfully and of his malice aforethought did kill and murder Squash-e-lek, Shil-at-ti-nord, Que-en and the female infant, to the Juror's unknown, against the peace of Our Lady the Queen, her crown and dignity."[38] Peter was returned to Nanaimo and confined in the gaol underneath the Bastion. On Friday, March 10, 1869, he was hanged.

Peter's life may have come to an end, but his "journey" was far from over. It is believed that because Peter was neither Caucasian nor First Nations, both groups opposed his being buried in their cemeteries or on their lands. As a result, he was interred in an unmarked grave at his last place of freedom—the bay on the east side of Newcastle Island, now known as Kanaka Bay. Here Peter rested quietly until October 4, 1899, when workers for the New Vancouver Coal Mining and Land Company, developing a new mine shaft inland from Kanaka Bay, uncovered a well-preserved casket which was found to contain a skeleton. The leather shoes that encased the feet were in a good state of preservation. A coroner's inquest brought to light the forgotten story of Peter and the axe murders 30 years before. The *Nanaimo Free Press* reported that Peter's remains were again returned to Kanaka Bay—to yet another unmarked grave.

Today this grisly story still brings chills and shudders, and it remains a favourite campfire yarn at Newcastle Island Provincial Marine Park. Tales of Peter's ghost, nightly stalking the campground, have been known to suppress the youthful exuberance of raiding parties at Wolf Cub and Brownie camps.

*Japanese fishers used twin boats to seine herring in Departure Bay, c.
1910. The white building near the shore to the left is the current Annex of
the Pacific Biological Station.*

*The photo below was taken from the summit of Sugarloaf Hill in 1912.
You can see the saltery in Sunset Bay. Shortly after this photo was taken
these salteries were destroyed by a fire of suspicious origin.*

CHAPTER 8

SALTED HERRING

Exactly when the first Japanese arrived in Nanaimo and when they first established a fishing community on Newcastle Island is unknown. However, by the late 1800s, their presence in British Columbia was well established and their influence on the provincial fishing industry was considerable. By the turn of the century they controlled a large portion of the provincial salmon and herring fisheries. During this era, Japanese fishers established their presence in the area now known as Saltery Beach on the Departure Bay side of Newcastle Island.

As the establishment of new salteries and the expansion of the old continued on Newcastle Island, the success of the Japanese resulted in

strong hostility among some members within the White community. On July 12, 1912, four salteries were destroyed by fire, with an estimated loss of $21,000. The owners of these salteries were all Japanese Canadians: Mr. Makino; Mr. Shinobu; and Mr. Mase and Mr Oburi (Mitsuru Shimpo, personal communication). Arson was suspected but never proven, and these facilities were quickly rebuilt.

The prime markets for salted herring were Japan, Hong Kong, and Mainland China, and both Japanese and Chinese immigrants played a role in the Nanaimo fishery. In 1918, Vancouver businessman T. Matsuyama (see insert block) joined the Ode brothers by investing $200,000 to develop a ship-building and repair shop at their herring camp on Newcastle Island. This facility was named Nanaimo Shipyards Limited.

Steveston on the Fraser River was the home of the first herring saltery in British Columbia, and Nanaimo was the home of the second. By the early 1920s, 43 Japanese herring salteries successfully operated in the Greater Nanaimo area, prompting a popular movement to designate the city "herring town" rather than "coal town." Nanaimo Ship-

T. MATSUYAMA

T. Matsuyama arrived in British Columbia near the turn of the century and established himself as a successful businessman in Vancouver. In later years, Rutaro Kita became secretary-treasurer of the T. Matsuyama Company. Its prime investments centred on fishing vessels and the fishing industry. In 1918, Matsuyama invested the then-considerable sum of $200,000 to establish Nanaimo Shipyards Limited for the building and repairing of ships on Newcastle Island. In 1941, with the internment of all Japanese resident in coastal British Columbia, Matsuyama chose to return to Japan on a Red Cross exchange boat. Having lost the empire he built, disappointed but not hostile, he said to his friends: "I came to this country with one kori [a wicker basket], (Jim Sawada, Nelson, BC, to Bill Munn, April 7, 1980, personal communication). I am going back with one kori. I haven't lost anything!" In 1953, Matsuyama returned to Vancouver.

yards Limited grew to employ 8 carpenters year round, plus 3 or 4 more in the busy season; 12 painters/labourers; 3 kitchen workers; and 3 occidental machinists/mechanics. By 1939 the main shop was 80 feet by 80 feet (24 by 24 metres) with 4 marine ways. Behind the camp was a

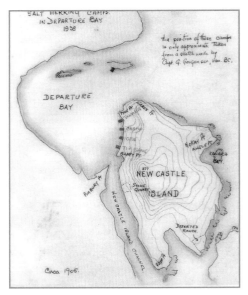

Sketch made by Capt. G. Gorgensen, of Vancouver, B.C. showing the approximate location of the four salteries in operation on Newcastle Island in 1938.

fresh-water well, a small orchard, and vegetable gardens (see photo p. 93). At this time three other herring salteries were also on the Departure Bay side of Newcastle Island: two were Japanese-owned (Mr. Tanaka and Mr. Kasho, personal correspondence) and one was Chinese-owned (Won Sang) (J. W. Sawada, personal correspondence).

Fishing vessels built on Newcastle Island included the seiners *Departure Bay 1*, *Departure Bay 2*, and *Departure Bay 3* (Graham Elliston, personal correspondence). The first two were designed and built by Mr. Arimoto, while the third (visible in photo) was build by Jitaro Sawada. In 1941 Nanaimo Shipyards owned 16 boats (J. W. Sawada, personal correspondence). Due to their season, both salmon and herring could be salted for shipment at the same facilities. The salmon season ran six weeks, from early July until mid-August, and the herring season ran from December through February. During the 1920s, the herring season was extended when it was decided to begin it in September (Mitsuru Shimpo, personal correspondence).

The prime method the Japanese used for seining herring involved the employment of two boats. These were built as twins, with one strengthened on the port side, the other on the starboard side. They would surround a school of fish and then come together to complete the purse. Back at the saltery, the herring were packed in salt—500 pounds (227 kilograms) to a box—for shipment. Basically, the Japanese salteries were large sheds built on piles. Unlike most other salteries, the side walls of Japanese salteries were open. All the work, from unloading the fish on arrival to boxing them for shipment, was done manually. The workers lived in buildings onshore.

Nanaimo pioneer John Allan recalls that he worked for Ode at his Japanese-style salting works on Newcastle Island. At that time a quota of

Whites and Japanese working in the depression-era fishing industry was being regulated by the British Columbia Salt Fish Board under the federal Natural Products Marketing Act. This decision-making board was made up of seven members, consisting of five Whites and two Japanese Canadians. They not only established the annual fishing quotas, but also assured that a certain number of White and First Nations fishers (up to 50 per cent) were employed at the Japanese Canadian salteries.

John Allan remembers the Ode saltery as being occupied only during the fishing season. Through the summer, notwithstanding the presence of a watchman, the camp was largely unoccupied. Pay was 45 cents per hour, and employees were given a 10-minute coffee break mid-morning and mid-afternoon, respectively. A break of this nature was unheard of in other fish camps of the period. Between 25 and 30 workers lived at Ode's fishing camp during the season, with additional workers being ferried in by boat when needed. Whites who worked for Ode had considerable praise for his management practices and the personal treatment he afforded them.

With the 1941 outbreak of hostilities with Japan, Canada's government felt compelled to take unprecedented action. All persons of Japanese ancestry were interned and moved to the BC Interior, some as far as the Kootenays. The Custodian of Enemy Alien Property confiscated all Japanese private property that the internees could not carry. Good fish boats were sold in Vancouver for $300. The seiners *Departure Bay 3* and *Departure Bay 5* (owned by Nanaimo Shipyards Limited) were among those purchased by Nelson Brothers Fisheries Limited (Vancouver) in 1942 (Graham Elliston, personal correspondence).

On Newcastle Island, Nanaimo Shipyards Limited and 4.18 acres (1.69 hectares) of land was taken over by the Royal Canadian Navy for use as a wartime repair depot for small vessels. This depot was under a 21-year lease from the Canadian Pacific Railway, the owners of Newcastle Island. Workers were ferried over to the base from Departure Bay.

At the end of the Second World War the Custodian of Enemy Alien Property sold all the Japanese facilities on Newcastle Island for $3,500. The purchaser was instructed to sell, dismantle, and clear everything. What could not be sold or removed was burned. Number 2 shipway was purchased by John Rowan in 1945 and moved south, along Newcastle Island Passage. This was the start of the present-day Nanaimo Shipyards Limited on Stewart Avenue. Number 1 shipway was purchased by Jim's Boatworks, which became Robertson's and is now no longer in business.

Today signs of the saltery operations are quite prevalent. Some construction was undertaken during the navy's presence (visitors can still find a cement block with July 1943 etched into it). Most of the remains, however, date back to the Japanese presence. The shipways, building footings, pile bases (visible only at low tide), a steam-generation boiler, and shards of broken pottery along the beach are visible reminders of this once-thriving industry. They are also a sad reminder of innocent British Columbians who lost their livelihood and possessions, victimized by war.

BILL MUNN

In 1980, as part of the preparation for the Newcastle Island Provincial Park Master Plan, 1983, Bill Munn, BC Park Planner in the Nanaimo Regional Office, made a concerted effort to research the history of the Japanese fishing community that operated off Newcastle Island. Bill made contact with a number of families that had either lived or worked on the island. Primarily, these  were employees of Ode and the Nanaimo Shipyards Limited. The assistance given Bill by Jim Sawada of Nelson, George Hamagami of Vancouver, and Mrs. Takenaka of Vancouver was extremely important. Bill's detailed notes provided a major contribution to the understanding of this fascinating chapter in Newcastle Island's history. Although his work was never put into report form, his research was kept together and made available to me. With the closing of the BC Parks Regional Office in Nanaimo, Bill and his family relocated to Victoria, where he continues his career as a planner with BC Parks.

The collection of Schwarze photographs on the following pages is representative of the historic contribution the Schwarze family has made to the community.

Counter-clockwise from top left the photos show:

1. *Brechin Point, Newcastle Island, and three of the four salteries present, c. 1937.*
2. *Herring being brought on shore for salting. Notice the dogfish in the nearest enclosure.*
3. *Japanese fishers with a set of herring in Departure Bay.*
4. *Workers both White and Japanese along with their wives at the Ode Brothers camp on Newcastle Island. The fishing vessel behind the group is believed to be the seiner, Departure Bay 3.*
5. *Workers salting herring, c. 1937.*
6. *Herring saltery sheds in Nanaimo Harbour, c. 1935.*

Looking across Departure Bay from near Brechin Point showing the saltery buildings in the background, with Japanese fishers actively seining herring by their unique double vessel method.

Digging clams with children playing in the tide pool beyond. The shipways to the Ode Brothers ship building and repair facility are to the right of this picture.

The view looking south along Saltery Beach from near Tyne Point. Notice the pilings of the most northerly Saltery projecting above the water.

Part of the residential and working space of the Japanese when they were in residence on Newcastle Island. See the series of pilings to the left that were once the supports to one of the large saltery sheds.

CHAPTER 9

COMMUNICATION TO VANCOUVER

If you drive down Brechin Road hill towards the BC Ferries Terminal, a distinct cleft is apparent in the trees on Newcastle Island. Though this gap is now filling in, it is still a visible reminder of the one-time telephone cable link between Nanaimo and Vancouver. The first telephones in Nanaimo were built in 1877 by Mr. Wall, a mechanic at Wellington Collieries. As a personal interest, and following what he had read about Alexander Graham Bell's invention, Wall assembled the materials and put together Nanaimo's first two telephones. Crude by present-day standards, these two phones were connected by a line from the North Wellington mine pit-head to the loading wharf on Departure Bay. Robert Dunsmuir, the mine owner, was very pleased with Wall's ingenuity and wanted more telephones. Potential patent infringement, however, precluded Wall's furthering his enterprise. So on his next visit to San Francisco, Dunsmuir purchased several telephones for his business.

According to information supplied by John Cass, the Nanaimo Telephone Company was formed in 1887, at which time it had eight subscribers. Anyone having a telephone was known as a "telephone crank." By 1901 the Nanaimo system was connected to Victoria and, in February 1905, the British Columbia Telephone Company absorbed the Nanaimo Telephone Company.

In June 1911 it was announced that the world's longest telephone cable would soon connect Nanaimo with Vancouver. Captain A. R. Richardson of the Pacific Coast Cable Company was to supervise the laying from Vancouver's Point Grey to Kanaka Bay on Newcastle Island

and then overland to Nanaimo. Local resident Wilf Cain recalls that "to span the 1,000-foot breadth of Newcastle Island Passage the cable was suspended from double poles with a cross arm 70 feet (21 metres) high on Newcastle and 110 feet (33 metres) high on the Brechin Point Side" (Wilf Cain, personal communication). Even at this height sailing ships still had to be careful not to get their top-gallants caught in the cable at high tide. The *Nanaimo Free Press* announced the completion of this project on June 16, 1913. It was the first time such a cable had been laid across a sea-floor without a break or a joint.

At Kanaka Bay, where the cable came ashore, a small hut marked the terminus. The concrete pad for this structure is still visible mid-trail. The concrete-encased bases of the 70-foot poles on the west side of Newcastle Island can still be seen if one looks carefully along Passage Trail.

Improvements in telephone systems continued. In 1927 new submarine cables were laid that not only improved service from Nanaimo to Vancouver but were also part of the great around-the-world telephone/ telegraph system. This cable crossed Vancouver Island to Port Alberni, to the Bamfield Cable Station, and then across the Pacific Ocean to Australia. The section of cable that crossed Newcastle Island Passage was removed and replaced by a submarine cable in October 1930. At this time, advances in technology allowed radio and telephone communication to bypass the use of cables. With the development of transmitting and receiving stations, the need for cables disappeared. As the facilities on Newcastle Island were no longer required, nature began to reclaim the telephone right-of-way—a process that is not yet complete.

Insulators seen along some of the trails, particularly the Kanaka Bay Trail, are from the days of the Canadian Pacific Railway resort. It seems

likely that this system tapped into the cable at Kanaka Bay. Like so many of the chapters in Newcastle Island's history, the island's once important role has been eclipsed, in this instance by technology. Today, all we are able to observe is a small remnant of the days when all telephones were connected by wires.

A portion of the telephone line that stretched across Newcastle Island from Nanaimo to Kanaka Bay.

P.O. Box 221   Nanaimo, B.C.

The RELIABLE BOAT HOUSE

Corner Wharf and Front Streets

• • • • • • • • • •

Row Boats, Canoes and Launches for sale
or hire.

Boats Bought and Sold.

Launch Trips to Any of the Islands

RATES REASONABLE

• • • • • • • • • •

MRS. H.C. ANDERSON, PROP.

In the 1920s Mrs. Anderson's Reliable Boat House (see advertisement above), often simply referred to as Anderson's, was a Nanaimo institution. This family operation rented row boats (single and double sets of oars), Peterborough canoes, and motor boats from its facility in the present-day Nanaimo boat basin, below the Coast Bastion Hotel. During the 1920s and 1930s, it was a common practice to row or paddle across the harbour to Newcastle Island. The Andersons had about a dozen canoes (which were rented for 50 cents per hour) and between 15 and 20 row boats (which were rented for 25 cents per hour for a single and 35 cents per hour for a double). It was Anderson's that gave many Nanaimo people access to Newcastle Island.

Before the CPR resort was opened, the Anderson family also operated a seasonal ferry service to Newcastle Island (as well as to Protection and Gabriola Islands). The fare to Newcastle Island was 15 cents for children, 25 cents for adults. Previous to the Andersons, Thomas MacKay ran a similar service. Much of the ferry traffic was made up of people heading for weekend church, lodge, and community organization picnics (Marcial Galloway, personal communication).

CHAPTER **10**

UNDER THE HOUSE FLAG OF THE CANADIAN PACIFIC RAILWAY [39]

In 1925 the Canadian Pacific Railway (CPR) began looking for a suitable site in which to expand its summer excursion party business. Company correspondence of that time states that the primary requirements for such a site were "close proximity to Vancouver, good bathing facilities, ample level ground for sports, shady spots for picnic tables and plenty of fresh water." One of the first locations investigated was 97 acres at Taylor Bay, on Gabriola Island.[40]

This was the era before automobiles and an extensive system of paved roads was readily available. Horses were still a common sight on Vancouver streets, and the average Vancouver family had limited means of "getting away." The idea of a recreational escape for a day or a weekend, as provided by the Union Steamship and Harbour Navigation Companies, was a very attractive and reasonably priced proposition. A day cruise to an "exotic" or popular destination was the "in" thing. In some instances overnight and/or weekly accommodation was also available.

In the 1920s the CPR was a large and powerful organization with worldwide transportation and shipping interests. From Vancouver, it operated the British Columbia Coast Steamship Service (BCCSS), which served the sheltered inland waters with their Princess ships. This international fleet of Empress ships plied the oceans of the world.

The rivalry between the companies offering excursion steamship services to locations within easy reach of Vancouver was intense. The Sunshine Coast and Howe Sound were the acclaimed domain of the Union Steamship Company which, in 1921, had purchased 1,000 acres on Bowen

Pier D of the Canadian Pacific Railway's steamship service as it appeared in Vancouver in 1925. Princess ships are on this side and one of the Empress boats is on the other. This is where passengers would embark from Vancouver for Newcastle Island.

The front panel of the 1931 CPR's brochure. Who was P.— the graphic artists?

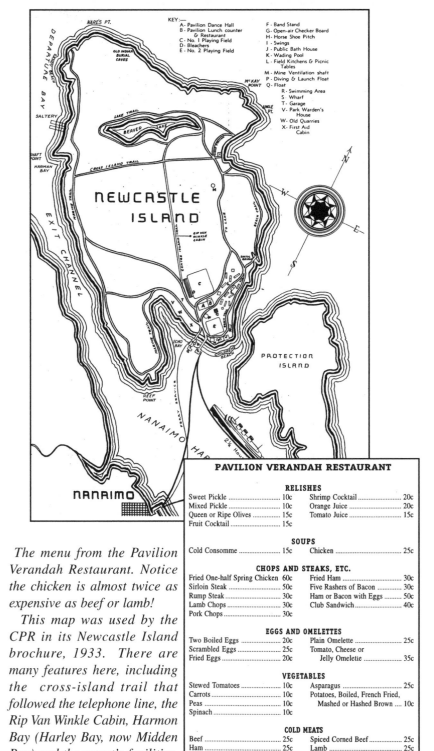

KEY:—
A - Pavilion Dance Hall
B - Pavilion Lunch counter & Restaurant
C - No. 1 Playing Field
D - Bleachers
E - No. 2 Playing Field
F - Band Stand
G - Open-air Checker Board
H - Horse Shoe Pitch
I - Swings
J - Public Bath House
K - Wading Pool
L - Field Kitchens & Picnic Tables
M - Mine Ventilation shaft
P - Diving & Launch Float
Q - Float
R - Swimming Area
S - Wharf
T - Garage
V - Park Warden's House
W - Old Quarries
X - First Aid Cabin

NEWCASTLE ISLAND

DEPARTURE BAY
NARE'S PT.
OLD INDIAN BURIAL CAVES
McKAY POINT
ANGLE PT.
SALTERY
SHAFT POINT
HARMON BAY
BEAVER LAKE
LAKE TRAIL
CROSS ISLAND TRAIL
RIP VAN WINKLE CABIN
EXIT CHANNEL
REEF POINT
ECHO BAY
PROTECTION ISLAND
NANAIMO HARBOUR
NANAIMO
2¼ Hour

The menu from the Pavilion Verandah Restaurant. Notice the chicken is almost twice as expensive as beef or lamb!

This map was used by the CPR in its Newcastle Island brochure, 1933. There are many features here, including the cross-island trail that followed the telephone line, the Rip Van Winkle Cabin, Harmon Bay (Harley Bay, now Midden Bay) and the resort's facilities.

PAVILION VERANDAH RESTAURANT

RELISHES

Sweet Pickle	10c	Shrimp Cocktail	20c
Mixed Pickle	10c	Orange Juice	20c
Queen or Ripe Olives	15c	Tomato Juice	15c
Fruit Cocktail	15c		

SOUPS

Cold Consomme	15c	Chicken	25c

CHOPS AND STEAKS, ETC.

Fried One-half Spring Chicken	60c	Fried Ham	30c
Sirloin Steak	50c	Five Rashers of Bacon	30c
Rump Steak	30c	Ham or Bacon with Eggs	50c
Lamb Chops	30c	Club Sandwich	40c
Pork Chops	30c		

EGGS AND OMELETTES

Two Boiled Eggs	20c	Plain Omelette	25c
Scrambled Eggs	25c	Tomato, Cheese or	
Fried Eggs	20c	Jelly Omelette	35c

VEGETABLES

Stewed Tomatoes	10c	Asparagus	25c
Carrots	10c	Potatoes, Boiled, French Fried,	
Peas	10c	Mashed or Hashed Brown	10c
Spinach	10c		

COLD MEATS

Beef	25c	Spiced Corned Beef	25c
Ham	25c	Lamb	25c
Tongue	25c	Chicken	40c

Island and had promoted it as "the playground of Vancouver." The company built a dance pavilion that was said to accommodate 800 couples, and its Bowen Island recreation complex started the era of British Columbia's interest in island pleasure resorts.

Given the success of the Union Steamship Company at Bowen Island and Selma Park (near Sechelt), and of the Harbour Navigation Company at Belcarra, the CPR felt greatly handicapped by not having its own excursion destination. Despite the stock market crash of the prior year and signs of a worsening depression, in 1930 CPR purchased Newcastle Island from the Western Fuel Corporation of Canada for $30,000. By April 1931 work on clearing the site had begun. No worker was being paid less

NEWCASTLE: A PLACE FOR PICNICS THEN AND NOW

Beginning in 1913, on any given Saturday in July as many as 1,500 Nanaimo and District coal miners, their families, and friends attended the annual Miner's Picnic on Newcastle Island. In the early years a scow, powered by the tug *Wee Two*, would ferry the miners across the harbour. The cost of this picnic was shared by the miners and mine owners. Participants played horseshoes, baseball, and rugby; ice cream and drinks, including beer, were free.[41] After the picnic it is said that some "stragglers" from these joyous festivities forgot they were on an island and had a difficult time finding their way home.

From 1973 until it disbanded in 1989, the Coal Tyee Society rejuvenated the memory of the earlier Miner's Picnic with "Coal Tyee Days." In part its purpose was to rekindle the memory of Nanaimo's coal-mining past and to support the research that led to the publication of Lynne Bowen's acclaimed books *Boss Whistle* and *Three-Dollar Dreams*. Although the coal-mining period on Newcastle Island ended nearly a century earlier, the island remained the place where coal miners wished to gather for social occasions.

Newcastle Island has always been considered Nanaimo's "private" playground. Even when the CPR resort was in full operation and thousands of picnickers arrived on site, Nanaimoites got to Newcastle Island ahead of the excursion ships. Not being limited by the CPR sailing schedule, these people had first access to the resort facilities and so took the best picnic tables and claimed the best locations.

than 50 cents per hour for an eight-hour shift. Included in the construction was a dance pavilion, a restaurant, sport grounds, and picnic and sanitary facilities. Water and electricity were brought to the island from Nanaimo. The CPR's investment in Newcastle Island exceeded $100,000. The main contract was awarded to the Victoria Pile Driving Company, and Douglas McGary directed the project. J. M. Cameron was in charge of administration and on-site supervision. When construction was completed, the resort was turned over to the CPR's Coastal Steamship Service.

The designer of the CPR Pavilion is not known but was likely from Victoria, where the contract managers had their headquarters. It is also possible, however, that CPR personnel were responsible for the design. The pavilion, 130 feet long and 40 feet wide, was the focal point of the resort. A wide veranda provided additional space, where meals and tea could be taken. The pavilion also served as shelter during inclement weather, and on summer evenings the veranda was open for outdoor candlelight dining. Large shutters on the outside walls could be raised, permitting summer breezes and unobstructed views across the grounds.

The west half of the pavilion contained a dance hall, which included a small orchestra stage; the east half contained a soda fountain, lunch counter, and two restaurants. The pavilion restaurant served meals *table de hote*, while the Veranda Restaurant served meals *a la carte*. The cooks were from Canton and Hong Kong, brought to British Columbia via the CPR's international Empress service. High-school girls from Nanaimo were employed as waitresses.

On Saturday, June 20, 1931, the *Princess Victoria* brought 412 passengers from Victoria, and Dr. G. A. B. Hall, Mayor of Nanaimo, officially opened the resort. The CPR, hoping that large company picnics and civic groups would patronize its new resort, invited many prominent people and business executives from Vancouver, Victoria, and Nanaimo. The following Thursday, the *Princess Victoria* officially started a new summertime service, making the first direct trip from downtown Vancouver to Newcastle Island. Its sailing time was two hours and 19 minutes. The following Friday, the *Princess Victoria, Princess Patricia,* and *Princess Joan* arrived at Newcastle Island, carrying 2,551 passengers.[42] Included in this entourage were employees of the City of Vancouver and the Vancouver Civic Federation. All departments in the city's municipal government were represented.

While no overnight accommodations were provided on the island proper, the CPR soon anchored two of its older ships—the *Charmer* and the *Princess Victoria*—and used them as floating hotels. For as little as $7.50 per week, guests were provided shipboard accommodation. Meals could be purchased at the pavilion at moderate rates, or guests could prepare their own in the ship's galley.

The furnishings for the pavilion came from various divisions of the CPR and consisted, primarily, of surplus from the company's maritime shipping operations. Some of the ships that contributed furnishings were the SS *Sardonyx*, the *Princess Louise*, the *Princess May*, the *Amur*, and the *Princess Royal*. Light fixtures from the Hotel Vancouver and seats from dismantled Esquimalt and Nanaimo Railway cars also found new uses in and around the pavilion which, the *Vancouver Province* of June 26, 1932, observed, was "rapidly taking on the aspect of a museum of steamship history." Additional pavilion accoutrements included models (in longitudinal section) of CPR ships, pictures, and paintings (some of which were originals). The pavilion flew the Union Jack at one end and the CPR house flag at the other.

THE *CHARMER*

The *Charmer* had a most interesting past. Originally under American registry and named the *Premier*, it was involved in a serious collision in 1892. In a foggy Puget Sound, the coal freighter *Willamette* collided with the *Premier*, cutting her through to the keel and killing four passengers. The *Premier* was beached with massive damage, and court action followed. Due to its condition the *Premier* was not placed under arrest and, a few weeks later, was surreptitiously salvaged and towed into Canadian waters. Placed under Canadian registry and then repaired, the *Premier* became the *Charmer* and never again entered American waters. Two more accidents followed. In 1906 it was damaged by the tug *Sea Lion*, and in 1907 it collided with the CPR's *Tartar*. The 200-foot *Charmer* was the first vessel in British Columbia to be equipped with electric lights. It ended its career as a floating hotel at Newcastle Island before being broken up for scrap in 1935.[43]

In its first season—between June 20 and September 7, 1931—the CPR carried 14,323 passengers to Newcastle Island, and its total revenue was $21,762.35. While daily excursions from Vancouver were available, the company told reporters that weekday business "was not quite as much as we anticipated." Five special trips were made: two from Victoria, one from New Westminster, one from Cowichan Bay, and one evening dance cruise.[44]

Fore and aft, the Princess Victoria *(three funnels) and* Charmer *acted as boatels at one point in the resort's history. The* Princess Victoria *was moored at Newcastle from 1934-36 before being returned to service. Its last voyage was a return trip from Vancouver to Nanaimo in August 1950. The* Charmer, *pulled off Gulf Island service in 1933, tied up at Newcastle for a brief hotel career before being sold in 1935.*

Vancouver remained the primary source of visitors to the Newcastle Island resort, and both family and company picnics as well as moonlight cruises gained prominence. Also, excursions from Victoria, both by Princess ships and by rail (the Esquimalt and Nanaimo Railway), were inaugurated; however, in later years these diminished in importance.

Though the CPR used its Newcastle Island resort primarily for the purpose of generating passenger use on its coastal ferry service, the benefits to Nanaimo were considerable. Nanaimo businesses, entertainers, sports groups, and individuals supplied many of the resort's services and entertainment. Then came the Second World War.

With the outbreak of war, two Princess vessels, the *Princess Kathleen* and the *Princess Marguerite* (torpedoed and sunk in the Mediterranean in 1942) were requisitioned for war service. With war being the priority, the CPR was already losing money on its resort operation. In 1941 service to Newcastle Island was suspended; and by the time the war was over,

EARL MARSH

At the age of 16 Earl Marsh joined the CPR's British Columbia Coast Steamship Service (BCCSS) as an office boy. He later served on board the Princess ships *Mary, Marguerite, Kathleen, Louise,* and *Victoria* before becoming the BCCSS's assistant accountant and then the accountant in its Victoria Office. He was transferred briefly to Montreal and, in 1964, when the BCCSS moved its offices to Vancouver, Earl relocated to the Mainland until he retired and returned to Victoria in 1973.[45]

Earl's passion has long been the history of coastal steamship service in British Columbia. During his 49-year employment with the CPR's coastal steamship service, Earl saved many records, artefacts, and documents that were destined for the garbage dump. Copies of the CPR's Newcastle Island Resort correspondence, brochures, menus, and promotional advertising reproduced in this book are a small part of Earl's collection and a priceless record of this chapter of Newcastle Island history. Earl may have been nicknamed "the junk man," but if he had not saved these materials our knowledge of the island during the days of the BCCSS would be very poor indeed!

AND THE BAND PLAYED ON

From Nanaimo: The Pimlots, the Stu Storey Band
From Vancouver: Goodheart, the Vancouver Electric
Band, the Dal Richards Band, the Bar B Boys, the Marie
Abrams Novelty Orchestra, and the West Vancouver
Boys' Band. These were some of the bands that played
on Newcastle Island.

THE COMPANY PICNIC

Organizations that picnicked on Newcastle Island from 1931 to 1941:

International Order of Foresters

Vancouver Daily Province paperboys

Fraternal Order of Eagles

The Sons of England

The Amalgamated Civil Servants

Employees of the BC Telephone Company (Vancouver and Victoria)

Vancouver Daily Province Annual Picnic

Malkin's Best Foods

Native Sons and Daughters of British Columbia

United Brewing Company

Spencer's Department Store

Woodward's Department Store

Vancouver Longshoremen

Canadian Pacific Railway Social and Athletic Club

BC Electric Company

Picnics were the order of the day in the 1930s and early 1940s. Here a gathering of unknown participants at a picnic (left), BC Electric (top), Malkin's Best Foods (bottom). This photo has been enlarged and placed on the east wall of the pavilion.

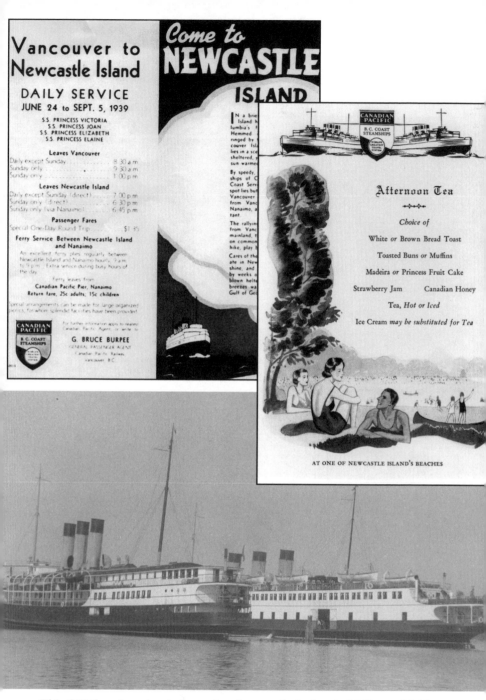

Vancouver to Newcastle Island

DAILY SERVICE
JUNE 24 to SEPT. 5, 1939

S.S. PRINCESS VICTORIA
S.S. PRINCESS JOAN
S.S. PRINCESS ELIZABETH
S.S. PRINCESS ELAINE

Leaves Vancouver

Daily except Sunday .... 8.30 a.m
Sunday only .... 9.30 a.m
Sunday only .... 1.00 p.m

Leaves Newcastle Island

Daily except Sunday (direct) .... 7.00 p.m
Sunday only (direct) .... 6.30 p.m
Sunday only (via Nanaimo) .... 6.45 p.m

Passenger Fares

Special One-Day Round Trip $1.35

Ferry Service Between Newcastle Island and Nanaimo

An excellent ferry plies regularly between Newcastle Island and Nanaimo hourly, 7 a.m to 10 p.m. Extra service during busy hours of the day.

Ferry leaves from
Canadian Pacific Pier, Nanaimo
Return fare, 25c adults; 15c children

Special arrangements can be made for large organized picnics, for whom splendid facilities have been provided.

For further information apply to nearest Canadian Pacific Agent, or write to

G. BRUCE BURPEE
GENERAL PASSENGER AGENT
Canadian Pacific Railway
Vancouver, B.C.

Come to NEWCASTLE ISLAND

Afternoon Tea

Choice of

White or Brown Bread Toast

Toasted Buns or Muffins

Madeira or Princess Fruit Cake

Strawberry Jam   Canadian Honey

Tea, Hot or Iced

Ice Cream may be substituted for Tea

AT ONE OF NEWCASTLE ISLAND'S BEACHES

This CPR brochure (top) shows that the round trip fare in 1939 was $1.35. The CPR "Afternoon Tea" menu as served at the pavilion. The Princess Victoria *and the* Princess Marguerite *tied alongside the wharf at Newcastle Island, c. 1938.*

tastes in recreation had changed. Automobiles, gasoline (no longer rationed), and paved roads provided access to new destinations and activities. Although the resort was briefly re-opened in 1950, it never regained its former popularity.

Three observations by BC historian Richard Mackie serve to summarize the historical significance of the CPR resort on Newcastle Island. First, the CPR Pavilion is the only surviving dance pavilion from the indigenous coastal resort industry that flourished in British Columbia between the two world wars. The resort artefacts are a tangible reminder of a pre-television era, when it was the custom to belong to groups and organizations that "did things together." Second, to the people of Nanaimo, Newcastle Island remains a primary recreational and social destination. The provincial park and its old pavilion are an important part of this city's culture and its historic link to an age of ships. British Columbia's coastal geography has long favoured sea-going access to both remote and not so remote communities. The establishment of the resort on Newcastle Island is a reflection and, in part, a reminder of this unique era in our province's maritime history. Third, the pavilion is a significant feature of the history of the CPR. It is a local remnant of an enormous transportation and hospitality network, operated by a very successful Canadian company, that played a major role in opening up the whole BC coast.

RIP VAN WINKLE— ON NEWCASTLE?

First published in 1819, Washington Irving's *The Sketch Book* introduced his readers to Rip Van Winkle. Rip's 20-year sleep upon consuming liquor served by little men must have caught the imagination of some CPR publicist. Printed in the CPR's Newcastle Island brochures for 1931 and 1932 is the location of Rip Van Winkle's cabin. This structure, to the east of the Centre Island Trail (now known as the Mallard Lake Trail) about half way between the CPR Pavilion and Mallard (then Beaver) Lake, was apparently an island attraction. No additional information on the cabin's origin has been found. Whether it was a fugitive's hide-out or the home of a recluse, does anyone know?

RICHARD MACKIE

In 1983 Richard was a graduate student in history at the University of Victoria. Anxious to gain writing experience and a summer job, he introduced himself to Don Tarasoff of BC's Heritage Trust, Ministry of Small Business, Tourism and Culture. Richard was asked to research and write a quick report and assessment on the old CPR Pavilion on Newcastle Island. To this he agreed. After a frenetic month of research and interviews, he concluded that the pavilion was the last surviving interwar dance hall on the coast and was, therefore, well worth preserving. Instead of being burnt to the ground, it was restored in 1984, thanks in large measure to Richard's research and the generous support of the Nanaimo Harbour Commission.

The momentum Richard gained from writing "The Newcastle Island Resort Pavilion, 1931-1941" propelled him towards a career of historical research and book writing. His latest book, *Trading Beyond the Mountains: The British Fur Trade on the Pacific Coast, 1793-1843*, was published in 1997.[46]

The swimming pier was the summertime hotspot, especially for the young.

CHAPTER 11

NEWCASTLE ISLAND POT-POURRI

Did any logging take place on Newcastle Island? The answer is both yes and no. Though the island was never logged in the sense that we understand it today, some selected logging took place to support the needs of the coal mines. Local pioneer John Allan recalls that, in the 1930s, members of the Chinese community horse-logged timbers for this purpose in and around the Midden Bay-Saltery Bay area. A little botanical detective work can verify this: cedar stumps with conspicuous springboard notches can still be found around the island.

Walking along trails today, one can find living Douglas fir stumps 20 to 30 centimetres in diameter that can de dated back to the horse-logging era. These stumps continue to live when the cut tree is naturally grafted by its roots to a nearby living tree. Although the stumps are without foliage of any kind, the root grafts allow them to behave like living trees in at least one respect: they grow a ring of new wood each spring. Eventually the flat cut surface of the stump disappears beneath a knarled dome of bark. By counting the rings back to the cut surface, the year in which the tree was logged can be determined. The poles cut by the Chinese were skidded out to Midden Bay by horse, boomed, and then towed to the site where they were processed for mine use.

From time to time larger timber was also taken to meet the special needs of the quarries and to carry telephone lines. In the 1980s, during the construction of sections of boardwalk, BC Parks used local fir to deck wet areas along trails. However, the impact of these incursions into the pristine island forests has been minimal. Today, BC Parks continues to remove dangerous trees and any windfalls that block trails. Such wood finds it way into the campground firewood supply.

Little is known of farming on Newcastle Island, but one 1904 map indicates that a ranch once operated on the field below where the pavilion stands today. It is believed that this farm was in operation from about 1880 until 1903. Although it has been suggested that this farm belonged to the Coundley family (John Allan, personal communication), Marcia Galloway, a great granddaughter of the Coundleys, rejects this. The original farmhouse stood near where the present CPR bath house now stands. When the air shaft at Kanaka Bay was under construction in 1899, this farm sold produce and dairy products to the work crews. After 1903 its owners relocated to Protection Island. The perimeter of this deserted farm is still visible, especially from a small plane. The border of the Douglas fir trees in front of the pavilion indicates the original boundary.

Newcastle Island has one other farming footnote. During the 1930s about 200 goats grazed here. Their reported purpose was to keep the underbrush down, and their sponsor was likely the CPR or the Western Fuel Company, who probably used them as a fire-control measure.

NEWCASTLE ISLAND: QUARANTINE STATION

Islands in the Gulf of Georgia have occasionally been used as quarantine stations. For example, D'Arcy Island, off the Saanich Peninsula, was, from 1891 until 1926, a leper colony. First run by the City of Victoria, after 1906 it was taken over by the federal government. In Nanaimo's early years, Newcastle Island served as a quarantine station for those with smallpox (and possibly other contagious diseases). Although inoculations were available at this time, not everyone received them.

The *Nanaimo Daily Free Press* (March 12, 1885) contains at least one account of Newcastle Island's use as a quarantine station. In early March, S. Grant Beaurup, age 22, was found to be suffering from smallpox and was removed from the Nanaimo Hotel and taken to Newcastle Island. Dr. Clueness, who was attending Beaurup, found that he had not been vaccinated. Beaurup died March 12 and, with the permission of S. M. Robins, Superintendent of the Vancouver Coal Mining and Land Company, was buried on Newcastle Island. Beaurup was survived by his parents in the United States. Where he was interred is not definitely known, but it is suspected that it was somewhere off the Kanaka Bay Trail. A letter dated April 6, 1885, from the city clerk of Nanaimo to Superintendent Robins expresses the city's regrets for accidentally burning down the house used during Beaurup's quarantine.[47] The accident occurred during fumigation, and the city offered compensation for the building's loss.

GIOVANDO LOOKOUT [48]

On October 12, 1986, the Nanaimo Gyro Club unveiled its dedication to the memory of their esteemed member, Dr. Larry Giovando, at Nares Point on Newcastle Island. Known as Giovando Lookout, the roofed structure commemorates Giovando's many contributions to his community. Born in nearby Ladysmith in 1905, he attended the University of British Columbia and the University of Oregon before earning his MD at McGill. He was founder of the Nanaimo Youth Council and the Nanaimo Sea Cadets, founding member of the John Howard Society, provincial MLA for his home riding from 1952 until 1956, CHUB Radio's 1962 recipient of "The Man Who Has Done Most For The Most People" award, and a long-time member of the Nanaimo Gyro Club. Giovando died in 1982, and this memorial recognized him for his selfless contribution and service to greater Nanaimo.

The modules for the lookout were prefabricated by inmates at the Brannen Lake Correctional Centre and helicoptered to the site for assembly. The architect of the $25,000 memorial was Ian Niamath of Nanaimo. Visitors to the lookout can gaze across Rainbow Channel, past Five Fingers and Hudson Rocks to the Coast Mountains and the Sunshine Coast, and imagine the Snuneymuxw's ancestors using this same site to watch for Lekwiltok raiding parties.

View from Giovando Lookout as it appears today.

MUNGO MARTIN
TOTEM POLES ON NEWCASTLE ISLAND

Mungo Martin was a noted Kwakiutl carver born at Fort Rupert, near present-day Port Hardy, in 1880 or 1881. After the death of his father, his mother remarried and Mungo became stepson to Charlie James, an innovative and powerful artist in the Kwakiutl style. Charlie James taught Mungo the art of carving. In the 1950s Chief Martin won wide acclaim while employed by the British Columbia Provincial Museum in Victoria. In a workshop open to the public, he did much of his later carving and took great strides "to secure recognition and honour for the culture of his people."[49]

In 1961, at the BC Parks workshop, Mungo Martin carved his final two poles, which were to be placed at Rebecca Spit Provincial Park on Quadra Island. However, what with the formal establishment of Newcastle Island Provincial Marine Park in October 1961 and the subsequent focus on a public celebration, these poles did not make it to their intended location. They remained at Newcastle Island until 1994, when they were removed, restored, and returned to a place of honour at Fort Rupert. In the interest of being appropriate to Snuneymuxw tradition, BC Parks has plans to replace the Mungo Martin poles with Coast Salish poles.

Chapter 12

Becoming a Park

With the closing of the resort after the failed CPR re-opening attempt in 1950, Newcastle Island became a recreational domain for the citizens of Nanaimo and its visitors. No longer did hordes of weekend picnickers arrive with the Princess vessels. While ships continued regular car and passenger services to Nanaimo, they no longer called at Newcastle Island. With no one taking an active role in island maintenance, buildings, recreation facilities, and established trails slowly began to deteriorate.

Through a referendum, the idea of purchasing Newcastle Island from the CPR was put to Nanaimo citizens on July 7, 1955. With a 60 per cent majority requirement, this referendum barely passed. The City Clerk's Office shows that there were 1,506 yes votes, 907 no votes, and 31 spoiled ballots. Nanaimo representatives entered into negotiation with the CPR for the purchase of Newcastle Island. The land value of the island was assessed at $100,000 plus $50,000 for improvements. While the City of Nanaimo paid the CPR $150,000 for Newcastle Island, its mineral rights remained with the Western Fuel Corporation of Canada and were not part of the sale.[50]

With 1,500 feet of dock space, Newcastle is a popular stopover for coastal boaters. It has no power or dockside facilities, but the island provides a wonderful overnight setting. Many boaters anchor in the inviting waters between Newcastle and Protection Islands.

Boaters using the wharf should take heed of the regular summer ferry that connects to Nanaimo. Stay clear of their space and try to position yourself so as to minimize the effect of their wakes. Mark Bay is also a popular anchorage, with good mud holding.

The city's financial plan was to borrow the money and pay off the principle over a period of 20 years. If taken to term, the full cost to Nanaimo, principle plus interest, would amount to $225,920. Four years later, maintenance costs and other financial obligations led the city to consider further options. On December 17, 1959, Nanaimo voters were asked the following question: "Are you in favour of Newcastle Island being taken over by the Provincial Department of Recreation and Conservation for dedication and development as a Provincial Park?" The response was 1,300 "Yes" to 197 "No"—86.8 per cent in favour.[51]

For the nominal price of one dollar and assumption of the mortgage, the province was asked to take possession of Newcastle Island on April 1, 1960. The City of Nanaimo's letter to the Honourable E. C. Westwood, Minister of Recreation and Conservation, requested "favourable assurance" on a number of issues regarding Newcastle Island, including access via a bridge as soon as feasible; a master development plan to be commenced forthwith; maintenance of facilities to the same or an improved degree. However, it was not on April 1, 1960, but on October 17, 1961, that Newcastle Island became a Class "A" provincial park. While one of the first marine parks, Newcastle Island was not *the* first: that honour went to Montague Harbour, on Galiano Island, in 1959.

The question of whether access from Nanaimo to Newcastle Island should be via bridge (at the cost of $200,000, as had been promised by Westwood), tunnel, or ferry has long been a local political issue. In 1995, a public advisory group to the master planning review process was unanimous in its resolve that, in order to maintain the park's environmental integrity, there should not be a bridge linking Newcastle Island to Nanaimo. This recommendation is now part of the park's access strategy.

Today, the focal point of Newcastle Island Provincial Marine Park remains the CPR Pavilion. An 18-unit campground, mooring facilities, a regular seasonal ferry service, and a well-maintained trail system ensure that the island continues its traditional role as Nanaimo's outdoor playground. To those who take the time to explore it, Newcastle Island is a true gem. The whole island is now protected as a provincial marine park, and it displays appropriate symbols of its past history. Fortunately, the incursion of development (first for coal mining; then for quarrying; then for fish processing and boat building; then, finally, for recreation) have enhanced rather than diminished Newcastle Island's fascination.

Getting to Newcastle Island in the summer months is an easy, economical experience for residents and visitors to Nanaimo. The waterfront "pirate statue," which pays tribute to longtime mayor Frank Ney, stands near the pier where paddlewheel boats leave for Newcastle.

Below, passengers on the Scenic Queen are treated to a short, pleasant journey through an armada of pleasure boats anchored between Newcastle and Protection Islands.

A FINAL COMMENT

My years of research on, and affiliation with, Newcastle Island have permanently bonded me to it. In thinking back through the events that have made Newcastle Island a special place for me, there are three things that stand out. The first is the great humility shown by T. Matsuyama when, in 1941, confronted by internment and forced to give up his considerable investments, he made the statement recorded in Chapter 8 ("I came to this country with one [suitcase], I am going back with one [suitcase]. I haven't lost anything!"). Perhaps his dignity should be recognised in some concrete way on the island itself. The second is the foresight, courage, and determination of the 1,506 residents of Nanaimo who, in 1955, voted to purchase Newcastle Island so that it might be preserved for all future generations. And the third is the Nanaimo Harbour Commission's decision (upon reading Richard Mackie's report) to finance the restoration of the CPR Pavilion, one of the island's crown jewels. Had the commission not come forward, who knows what Newcastle Island would look like today?

ENDNOTES

1. J. T. Walbran, *British Columbia Coast Names, 1592-1906: Their Origin and History* (Vancouver: Douglas and McIntyre, 1971).
2. Most likely a seasonal absence, as the Snuneymuxw moved to Gabriola Island each spring and then to the lower Fraser River in summer—the time of Pemberton's surveying activity. Pemberton's letter to Douglas is dated September 17, 1852.
3. Hudson's Bay Company Archives, report on coal seams at Nanaimo, including tracings of geological sections showing different strata. HBCA A.11/73 fos. 572-79 (includes a letter from J. D. Pemberton to James Douglas, Governor of Vancouver's [sic] Island).
4. Information on Newcastle Island Passage, Nares Point, Tyne Point, Shaft Point, McKay Point, and Nanaimo is taken from Walbran, *British Columbia Coast Names.*
5. Walbran, *British Columbia Coast Names,* 348.
6. Bruce F. Gurney, *The Geology of Nanaimo,* Adventures in Earth Science Series No. 18, 1977, Department of Geological Sciences, University of British Columbia, Vancouver, BC.
7. *Gazetteer of Canada*, 3rd edition (Ottawa: 1985).
8. John Allan, personal communication.
9. The information contained in this chapter relies on C. J. Yorath and H. W. Naysmith, *The Geology of Southern Vancouver Island: A Field Guide* (Victoria: Orca, 1995).
10. Ian R. Wilson and Susan Crockford, Public Archaeological Excavations at the Departure Bay Midden, DhRx 16, Permit 1992-29, 1992. (I. R. Wilson Consultants Ltd., Brentwood Bay, BC)
11. Walbran, *British Columbia Coast Names*, 348.
12. Franz Boas, "Notes on the Snanaimuq," *American Anthropologist* 2 (1889): 321-28.
13. The Southern Kwakiutl are part of the Kwak'wala-speaking peoples of northeastern Vancouver Island and the adjacent mainland. Today they are known as the Kwakwaka'wakw. Their traditional territory extended from about Kelsey Bay northward. Strictly speaking, the Kwakiutl is one band of the Kwakwakwa'wakw, who continue to live in and around the Port Hardy/Port McNeil area.

14. Grant Keddie, "Aboriginal Defensive Sites, Part 1: Settlements for Unsettling Times," *Discovery* 24 (December 1996/January 1997).
15. Boas, "Notes on the Snanaimuq," 321-28.
16. Beth and Ray Hill, *Indian Petroglyphs of the Pacific Northwest* (Saanichton: Hancock, 1974).
17. Charles Alfred Bayley, 1830-1889. "Early Life on Vancouver Island," BCARS E/B/B34.2, p. 6.
18. Randy Bouchard, "Notes on Nanaimo Ethnography and Ethnohistory," (Brentood Bay, BC: I. R. Wilson Consultants, 1993).
19. Robert Galois, *Kwakwaka'wakw Settlements, 1775-1920: A Geographic Analysis and Gazetteer* (Vancouver: UBC Press, 1994).
20. W. K. Lamb, "The Advent of the *Beaver*," *British Columbia Historical Quarterly* 2 (1938): 163-84.
21. Hudson's Bay Company, Nanaimo Correspondence, James Douglas to Joseph William McKay, 24 August 1852, BCARS.
22. Irene Spray, *The Palliser Expedition: An Account of John Palliser's British North American Expedition, 1857-1860* (Toronto: Macmillan, 1963).
23. John Palliser, *Papers relative to the Exploration of British North America, 1859-1865* (London: 1867), 216.
24. John Cass, *A Short History of Newcastle Island* (unpublished MS, 1983).
25. Don T. Sale, "Nanaimo's Princess Royal Day," *BC Historical News* 29 (1996): N.p.
26. Lynne Bowen, *Three-Dollar Dreams* (Lantzville: Oolichan, 1987).
27. Quoted in Cass, *History of Newcastle Island.*
28. Bowen, *Three-Dollar Dreams.*
29. William A. Parks, *Report on the Building and Ornamental Stones of Canada,* vol. 5 (Ottawa: Province of British Columbia, Mines Branch, 1917).
30. BC Parks, *A History of Newcastle Island Provincial Park* (Victoria: Historic Parks and Sites Division, Parks Branch, 1976). (Available through the BC Parks Branch Library, Victoria.)
31. William A. Parks, *Report on the Building and Ornamental Stones of Canada,* vol. 5 (Ottawa: Province of British Columbia, Mines Branch, 1917).
32. An undated *Nanaimo Free Press* article states: "The finest sandstone imported from England was used in the construction of this building."
33. Neil McDaniel, "Raising the Past," *Diver Magazine* 13 (January/February 1988): 18-19
34. Underwater Archaeological Society of British Columbia, *The Ship Zephyr: A Proposal* , 1984. Most of the information contained in Chapter 6 comes from this source.
35. Tom Koppel, *Kanaka: The Untold Story of Hawaiian Pioneers in British Columbia and the Pacific Northwest* (North Vancouver: Whitecap, 1995).

36. Mary Kawena Pukui, *Hawaiian Dictionary* (Honolulu: University of Hawaii Press, 1986).

37. *British Colonist*, February 17, 1869.

38. BCARS, GR 419, box 7, file 186912.

39. Unless otherwise indicated, the information contained in this chapter comes from Richard Mackie's 1983 report for the Heritage Conservation Branch, Province of British Columbia, entitled *The Newcastle Island Resort Pavilion, 1931-1941*.

40. Earl Marsh Collection, Canadian Pacific Railway Company correspondence 28 May 1926.

41. Lynne Bowen, *Boss Whistle* (Lantzville: Oolichan, 1987).

42. Earl Marsh Collection, Canadian Pacific Railway Company correspondence, 10 September 1931.

43. City of Vancouver Archives, *Port Watch: Historical Ships in Vancouver Harbour* (Vancouver: City Archives, 1986).

44. Earl Marsh Collection, Canadian Pacific Railway Company correspondence 10 September 1931.

45. Robert Turner, personal communication.

46. *Trading Beyond the Mountains: The British Fur Trade on the Pacific Coast, 1793-1843*, was published in 1997. Richard Mackie

47. Nanaimo Community Archives, City of Nanaimo, City Clerk's Letterbook, 1875-1886, p. 103.

48. The information contained in this section is taken from the *Nanaimo Times*, 9 October 1986.

49. Phil Nuytten, *The Totem Carvers: Charlie James, Ellen Neel, and Mungo Martin* (Vancouver: Panorama, 1982), 115.

50. B. Day, *Newcastle Island Park* (Victoria: BC Parks. 1977).

51. City of Nanaimo, correspondence dated 16 March 1960, file 1,018.

PHOTO CREDITS

p. 1   City of Vancouver Archives, OUT. P.377, N.127.

p. 10   Hudson's Bay Archives Map Collection, G.1/141 (N9463), Provincial Archives of Manitoba; BCARS A-01901.

p. 12   BC Information Management Services Map Collection CM/ B2444.

p. 12   BCARS C-08626.

p. 13   City of Nanaimo, Strategic Planning Section.

p. 17   BCARS # 01989.

p. 18   Courtesy Doreen Cowie.

p. 19   Nanaimo Museum and Archives.

p. 23   C. J. Yorath and H. W. Nasmith, *The Geology of Southern Vancouver Island: A Field Guide* (Victoria: Orca Book Publishers, 1995).

p. 24   Geological Surveys of Canada, "Nanaimo Coalfields, British Columbia, Map Paper 47-22.

p. 25   Ibid.

p. 27   Not available.

p. 28   Peter Schwarze, Schwarze Photographers, Nanaimo, BC.

p. 30   Royal British Columbia Museum, Victoria, BC, PN 1146.

p. 33   Bill Merilees.

p. 35   Peter Schwarze, Schwarze Photographers, Nanaimo, BC, Bill Merilees (bottom).

p. 38   Royal British Columbia Museum Photographic Collection, Negative PN 8959.

p. 39   BCARS F-04620, Nanaimo District Museum Archives.

p. 40   Hudson's Bay Company Archives Map Collection, Provincial Archives of Manitoba, G.1/140 (N4450), HBCA A.11/73 FOS 572-579.

p. 42   Not available (top), BCARS A-00578 (bottom).

p. 42   Frederick Claudet, Nanoose Bay, BC.

p. 43   BCARS F-05227.

p. 44   Wilf Hatch, courtesy Nanaimo Archives.

p. 45   B. Day, *Newcastle Island Park* (Victoria: BC Parks, 1977).

p. 47   BCARS.

p. 48   Peter Schwarze, Schwarze Photographers, Nanaimo, BC.

p. 54   Bancroft Library, University of California, Berkeley, CA., San Francisco Archives, San Francisco, CA., BC Parks Branch Library, Victoria, BC, Lynn Kerby.

p. 56   BCARS A-03358.

p. 57 BCARS B-04058, BCARS A-03928, Bill Merilees (bottom).

p. 59 Scott Crawford, Braeden Marketing.

p. 60 BCARS A-05891.

p. 62 BCARS E-5136 via BC Parks Library, Victoria, BC, Nanaimo Museum Archives, Number R-3-32.

p. 65 Fred Thirkell and Bob Scullion, *Postcards from the Past: Edwardian Images of Greater Vancouver and the Fraser Valley*, (Surrey: Heritage, 1996).

p. 66 BCARS A-00338.

p. 67 BCARS A-04631.

p. 68 Peter Schwarze, Schwarze photographers, Nanaimo, BCARS E-05128, BCARS E-05126 via BC Parks Library, Victoria, BC.

p. 69 BCARS F-08185, BCARS F-08192, BCARS F-08195.

p. 72 BCARS B-02499, BCARS C-03716.

p. 74 Heritage.

p. 77 Bill Merilees.

p. 79 BCARS PABC GR 419, Box 7, File 186912, BCARS, PABC GR 419, Box 7, File 186912, City of Vancouver Archives, ADD. MSS 782, Vol. 3, File 13.

p. 82 BC Parks Library, Victoria, BC.

p. 84 Peter Schwarze, Schwarze Photographers, Nanaimo, BC, City of Vancouver Archives, Cadieux Collection.

p. 87 Vancouver Archives, Cadieux Collection 782, Vol. 2, File 11.

p. 90 Peter Schwarze, Schwarze Photographers, Nanaimo, BC.

p. 91 Peter Schwarze, Schwarze Photographers, Nanaimo, BC.

p. 92 Nanaimo Museum Archives, U-2-16, Gary Moore, Newcastle Island Society.

p. 93 Gary Moore, Newcastle Island Society.

p. 95 BC Parks, Bob Ahrens, 1954.

p. 98 Vancouver Public Library No. 3119.

p. 99 Earl Marsh Collection.

p. 103 Nanaimo Museum Archives Q-3-14, Nanaimo Museum Archives Q-3-71.

p. 104 Earl Marsh Collection.

p. 105 Nanaimo Museum Archives L-62, Nanaimo Museum Archives L-68.

p. 106 BC Parks Library, Victoria, No. 00062.3.17.VI.

p. 107 Vancouver Public Library, No. 36462, No. 49293.

p. 108 Earl Marsh Collection (top), City of Vancouver Archives Pamphlet 1936-121 (middle), Peter Schwarze, Schwarze Photographers, Nanaimo, BC (bottom).

p. 111 Vancouver Public Library No. 36461, No. 36565-B, Harry Rafter.

p. 114 Bill Merilees.

p. 116 Heritage.

p. 117 Heritage.

p. 119 Bill Merilees.

INDEX

THE AUTHOR

Though primarily a student of natural history, Bill has long cultivated a secondary interest in local history. When the Merilees family resided in Castlegar Bill became the first president of the Kootenay Doukhobor Historical Society. In this capacity he was a primary force behind the reconstruction of a traditional Doukhobor Communal Village. On his arrival in Nanaimo in 1978, as an employee of BC Parks, the incredible history of Newcastle Island Provincial Marine Park came into focus. Using BC Parks, personal research, and the work of others, he compiled a vast treasure of information, much of which appears in this book.

Bill was born in Vancouver, a third-generation British Columbian. His post-secondary education was at the University of British Columbia, where he studied zoology and botany. With the help of a Rotary International Scholarship he completed a Master of Science degree at Colorado State University in outdoor education.

His first book *Attracting Backyard Wildlife* was published in 1989, and in 1995 with C.P. Lyons, he co-authored *Trees, Shrubs and Flowers to Know in British Columbia and Washington.*

Now retired from public service, Bill continues to reside in Nanaimo with his wife June, three sons, and a daughter. Writing, tour leading, travel, and a program of natural history research keep him busy, happy, and appreciative of Nanaimo's impressive resources.